"Proud To Be American"

Thomas R. Meinders

iUniverse, Inc.
Bloomington

"Proud To Be American"

iUniverse books may be ordered through booksellers or by contacting:

iUniverse
1663 Liberty Drive
Bloomington, IN 47403
www.iuniverse.com
1-800-Authors (1-800-288-4677)

ISBN: 978-1-4502-9872-8 (sc)
ISBN: 978-1-4502-9873-5 (dj)
ISBN: 978-1-4502-9874-2 (ebook)

Printed in the United States of America

iUniverse rev. date: 02/23/2011

INTRODUCTION:

The American Citizens Political Action Committee was founded to promote and sponsor candidates for offices throughout the United States that are committed to press for legislation that will benefit every citizen of the United States of America. The American Citizens PAC will work with groups of people that believe that America should return to our core values and the Constitution of the United States. As stated in the Gettysburg Address: "Government of the people, by the people, for the people, shall not perish from the earth." The time has come for all Americans to stand up and fight for what we want. It will be a tough battle but we can win if we all group together and express the policies that we believe are best for the United States. When we are a large enough group, the candidates for office will have to listen to our voice or they will not get elected.

The citizens of the United Stated that are concerned about the direction that our country has taken in the past few years need to act now. We can not afford to have any more spending bills passed into law.

Our beautiful country is bankrupt and will not admit the facts. Our deficit is going to ruin the lives of all our children and grand children. We just can not let this happen.

Act now and support our cause. Donations of any size will contribute to our success.

Do it now! Send your comments on what you would like to include in our newsletters to the representatives so that every American can be heard. Together we will return our government to the people. That is the way it should be. Government of the people, by the people, for the people, shall not perish from the earth.

Our primary focus will be to gain support from the candidates that will back the American Citizens PAC regarding immigration, amnesty, unemployment, taxes, deficits, energy policies, reduction in the size of government and other problems that are facing the United States. Our function will be to promote policies that the citizens of the United States are in favor of implementing and making sure that the candidates that are going to represent our districts will vote on what the citizen's desire and start listening to the voice of the people.

Our mission will be to have enough members and supporters that the 2012 elections will result in representatives that will be supporting our policies and by grouping together we can make a difference. We will be collecting feedback from citizens and then combining the input into what the majority of the citizen's desire on each of the different topics we will be debating.

Together we can make a difference. The big corporations have millions to sponsor programs that benefit the rich and corporate structure in America. The American Citizens can band together and raise millions to support our policies. By uniting and presenting our ideas to the candidates we will not be alone. Each of us would be fighting a loosing battle but together we can become a force that they will have to respect and listen to.

The American Citizens PAC will provide a complete listing of each and every one of the representatives in our government system. That will include the 535 members of Congress and the President. It will also include the representatives in each individual state so that everyone can be emailed with our opinions. If we decide to promote our policies instead of just saying to ourselves that our voice is only one and it will not make any difference. Together we can make a major difference. We can return the United States of America to the greatest country in the world and gain the respect of the world.

The input from our supporters we will determine which policies are having the greatest risk to the citizens of the United States. Immigration will be our original topic for input and it is critical to the stability of the United States. It is the largest threat to our economic conditions and the future of our country. We do not need Mexican Americans. Our founding fathers made it very clear that anyone that is to be a citizen of the United States must assimilate into our society and have respect for the American Flag and our heritage. They must speak our language which is English and become Americans. There are about 20,000,000 illegals in the United States at the present time. We must not allow our representatives in Congress or the President to vote for any type of amnesty for these illegals. Immigration into the United States has rules that must be followed to become an American and they must be followed.

Together we will be herd and we will get the results that we deserve. To track our progress you can log onto www.americancitizenspac.com any day and it will be updated regarding our progress.

THE FOLLOWING PROGRAMS ARE SUPPORTED BY THE AMERICAN CITIZENS POLITICAL ACTION COMMITTEE

INTRODUCTION: v

OVERVIEW OF THE AMERICAN CITIZENS PAC: xi

Chapter 1 — SECURING OUR BORDERS: 1

Chapter 2 — THE EFFECTS OF IMMIGRATION: 19

Chapter 3 — THE FEDERAL DEFICIT: 34

Chapter 4 — QUALIFICATIONS FOR CONGRESS...................45

Chapter 5 — OUR VAST NATURAL RESOURCES:.................58

Chapter 6 — EARMARK LEGISLATION...................................64

Chapter 7 — EARLY CAMPAIGNING: 68

Chapter 8 — GETTING AMERICANS JOBS 80

Chapter 9 — NO AMNESTY FOR ANYONE 92

Chapter 10 — THE UNITED STATES DECLINING
          ECOMOMY..100

Chapter 11 — THE TREND IN DEMOCRATIC POLITICS 115

Chapter 12 — THE LABOR UNIONS 130

Chapter 13 — DEFENSE SPENDING......................................134

Chapter 14 — THE NEXT RECESSION? 141

Chapter 15 — RESPECT FOR AMERICA: 159

Chapter 16 — ADDED FOOD FOR THOUGHT: 163

Chapter 17 — WHAT DO THE MEMBERS OF
                         CONGRESS SUPPORT?..181

ABOUT THE AUTHOR 187

OVERVIEW OF THE AMERICAN CITIZENS PAC:

The American Citizens Political Action Committee was founded to gather information on problem areas in our government that are being ignored. From the information that has been gathered to date it appears that we need to do some of the following to help correct the problems that are facing our cities, states and federal government and many more that we are going to face if our government at all levels do not start practicing better management policies. It is not too late to contact our representatives in all levels of government. If we do not take action now our children and grand children will be paying the rest of their lives for our mistakes. In addition, the way things are going they will be living in a third world country. I do not want to see that. Do You?

Contact your representatives and suggest to them that the American citizens want to see legislation that will address the following:

1. **Eliminate all of the entitlement programs that are providing support for the illegals that are in the United States.**

2. **Create laws that are enforced concerning businesses that hire illegals in the United States. Make the penalty $50,000 per offense. You will see an incredible number of jobs open up for the Americans.**

3. Make legislation that anyone that is on any type of entitlement program must pass a drug test on a monthly basis. If they do not pass the entitlements will be discounted immediately.

4. Create laws that are enforced concerning landlords that rent their properties to illegals. Make the penalty $25,000 per offense. You will see the landlords kicking the illegals out of their properties.

5. Complete the border fence and then enforce the immigration laws of the United States.

6. Enforce our laws about illegals entering the United States. There are about 1 million additional illegals each year.

7. Deport every illegal in the United States and that will free up about 10 million jobs for the Americans.

8. Pass legislation that the government presents a balanced budget each year. No more deficit spending.

9. No more spending unless there is a program to create income to cover the spending. The government can not go on living on a credit card.

10. Reduce the deficits at all levels of government.

11. Eliminate all pork projects known as earmarks.

12. Require all members of Congress and the President to pass a test to qualify for the office they are trying to occupy.

13. Make every member of Congress and the President to show proof that they have paid all income taxes.

14. Make every member of Congress and the President provides positive proof of citizenship and their educational background.

15. Pass legislation that makes English the language of the United States.

16. No more printing government forms and ballots in Spanish.

17. Eliminate the Department of Education. Return control of the schools (and their funding) to the states, counties, cities and towns where it belongs.

18. Eliminate the press 1 for English and just answer the phone in English. We do not need the press 2 for Spanish. Proud

Americans learn to speak the English language. It is a requirement for citizenship.

ACT NOW - WE ONLY HAVE A FEW MONTHS TO LOCATE THE REPRESENTATIVES THAT WILL ACT FOR THE BENEFIT OF ALL AMERICANS.

"PRIDE IN AMERICA"

I'm proud to be an American
I'm proud of the "Pledge of Allegiance"
I'm proud of the "National Anthem"
I'm proud to display the "American Flag"
I'm proud to defend the "American Freedoms"
I'm proud to communicate in "English"
I'm proud of freedom of "Religion"
I'm proud to be an American
God Bless the United States of America

Thomas R. Meinders

GOVERNMENT OF THE PEOPLE,

BY THE PEOPLE,

FOR THE PEOPLE,

SHALL NOT PERISH FROM THE EARTH.

PROGRAM ONE:

SECURING OUR BORDERS:

The most pressing policy that is facing the United States is securing our borders. Until we complete the security there will continue to be about 1 million illegals that are entering the United States every year. How can this country support all these people on our welfare and entitlement systems? The problem with these illegals is that they tend to be less educated and are taking thousands of construction jobs from our citizens. In addition, they end up in drug gangs and create violence where ever they end up. It is not unusual for them to have multiple families living in a small house. They are creating a drain on our state and local governments as well as the federal government. I believe we need to erect the border fence and build a highway running the length of the fence to enable our border patrol agents to monitor the illegals that are trying to enter the United States. What are the feelings of the American citizens?

BORDER POLICIES:

I do not know about the rest of American citizens but I do not want to put any threat into perspective. I want to know that my children and their children are going to be able to live in a safe and beautiful America. I hope that is what every American would like to see develop. I do not want the United States to develop into a third world country like some parts of the United States already have. Take back America.

It is not too late if we work together. Get involved while you can before it is too late. "God Bless America"

There is only one flag that should be flown in the United States of America and that is the American Flag. Every American should be very proud to fly this flag and respect what it stands for. The Pledge of Allegiance to the Flag of the United States should be recited every day by our schools to teach the values of our country and to be grateful for the freedoms that the United States provides. There is no other country so beautiful in the entire world. Be proud of America

THE NEWS YEARS JOKE OF THE YEAR FOR 2011....

You have to be kidding. The following was reported by the Associated Press on January 1, 2011. The United States will send more American experts to train the Afghan police and customs officials to better manage their porous border crossings.

Janet Napolitano says sending experts from the United States to train other countries on how to secure their borders. That is really something. Janet Napolitano does not have a clue about securing the borders. Look at the mess that the Department of Homeland Security has made of securing the southern borders of the United States. We do not have any border security so why would anyone want advice from the people that do not know what they are talking about? Get real and secure our own borders and let the Afghan's take care of their own borders. According to the Department of Homeland Security all you have to do is post a sign that it is dangerous in the area and the job will be done.

Napolitano said the United States would help Afghanistan with equipment and capacity building for the country's customs operations and with the training of border police. Why doesn't the Department of Homeland Security implement the policy of spending more money and equipment to defending the southern border of the United States of America?

For the past year, Napolitano's department has been working with the

Afghan government to establish a border security and customs system and crack down on the smuggling of drugs and cash. Last year was by far the deadliest for foreign troops in the decade-old war, with 702 killed, eclipsing the 2009 record of 504? The Department of Homeland Security should compare the total losses in combat in Afghanistan to the losses in one city just across the border from El Paso, Texas where there were 3,111 people killed in 2010 alone. Where are the real risks? This is just across the river from the United States.

The government needs to accept the facts and initiate immediate action to deploy our troops to the border and protect the United States.

Mexican city across the border from El Paso, Texas had 3,111 murders in 2010. It is getting real close to the United States and needs to be stopped. We need to secure our borders now before it is too late.

CIUDAD JUAREZ, Mexico – The embattled border city of Ciudad Juarez had its bloodiest year ever with 3,111 people killed in drug violence, an official said Saturday.

The city across from El Paso, Texas, has seen its homicide rate soar to one of the highest in the world since vicious turf battles broke out between gangs representing the Juarez and Sinaloa cartels in 2008.

That year, 1,587 people were killed in drug violence, and the toll increased to 2,643 in 2009.

Ciudad Juarez's bloodiest month last year was October, when 359 people were killed, said Arturo Sandoval, a spokesman for prosecutors in Chihuahua state where the city is located.

More than 33,000 people have been killed in drug violence nationwide since President Felipe Calderon launched an offensive against the cartels after taking office in December 2006.

Our government can not see the forest for the trees. The United States spends about $5.9 billion annually at the southern border; which by the way, is less than California and Texas spend combined just feeding and providing medical care to illegals immigrants annually. Securing the border would cost far less than the states and the federal governments spend on caring for illegals.

What about the illegals coming into the United States from the Canadian border? Not too likely that the illegals will fly or boat into Canada and cross the border. And, if you are concerned about Muslim terrorists, that we all should be, crossing the border for them is too much work. They easily fly right on into the United States every week on student and humanitarian visas. Look at how many Somalis have emigrated to Minnesota and register for government benefits and silently go about their business.

These types of activities are coming to cities in the United States as the violence continues to go without being stopped. We could very easily send our troops to defend our southern border. Why are we wasting billions of dollars trying to defend the borders of Afghanistan? The President has already stated the withdrawal date to leave Afghanistan. That bothers me since I was taught that if we entered a war it was to win at all costs. We have been in Afghanistan for about 10 years and then all of the sudden under President Obama we are packing it in and leaving. Why haven't our troops been given the authority to utilize our military strength and win this war? The United States does not need to be a police action military. When we enter a war it is to win. Nothing else will do.

What is the underlying reason that our government will not defend our borders? Is it because the party in power does not want to alienate the Hispanic voters? We need to start thinking about every American instead of a select block of voters. What ever happened to legislation and enforcement that will secure all the Americans? How many of the million illegals that enter the United States every year through the southern borders are terrorists? That is a question that our Department of Homeland Security will not answer. The United States should admit that we have been invaded and have not done anything to stop the invasion. The only difference is that this invasion was not accomplished with military troops. What difference is there in people trying to take over parts of our country and change the way of life in that part. It is not the American way. Have our troops defend our borders and stop this insult to all Americans.

THE DEMOCRATS JUST DO NOT GET THE MESSAGE:

Here we go again. On January 14, 2011 the following article was published concerning our southern borders. When will the President and the Department of Homeland Security get their heads out of the desert sand and accept the fact that the American citizens want a secure border and the only way to accomplish that is to complete a real fence. Not some virtual fence or any other type of space age technology that the Mexicans will be able to figure out on the first day it is in operation.

United States ends "virtual fence" project on Mexican border

By Jeremy Pelofsky Jeremy Pelofsky – January 14, 2011

WASHINGTON (Reuters) – President Barack Obama's administration on Friday canceled the troubled "virtual fence" project meant to better guard stretches of the vast U.S. border with Mexico and will replace it with other security measures.

The project, begun in 2006 and run by Boeing Co, has cost about $1 billion and was designed to pull together video cameras, radar, sensors and other technologies to catch illegal immigrants and smugglers trying to cross the porous border.

Homeland Security Secretary Janet Napolitano said commercially available surveillance systems, unmanned aerial drones, thermal imaging and other equipment would be used instead, suggestions made by critics of the Boeing SBInet program.

"This new strategy is tailored to the unique needs of each border region, providing faster deployment of technology, better coverage, and a more effective balance between cost and capability," she said in a statement.

The Obama administration has been under intense pressure to beef up security to stem the flow of illegal immigrants flooding across the U.S.-Mexico border as well as halt the smuggling of drugs and weapons.

Last year, Obama signed a $600 million bill to fund some 1,500 new

Border Patrol agents, customs inspectors and law enforcement officials along the border, as well as pay for two more unmanned drones.

Additionally, he ordered some 1,200 National Guard troops to the southwest border to help with security.

The SBInet project has faced setbacks, missed deadlines and cost overruns. The future of the project has been in doubt for some time after criticism by lawmakers and Napolitano.

"The SBInet system is not the right system for all areas of the border and it is not the most cost-effective approach to secure the border," the Department of Homeland Security said in its assessment of the project. It did note that some of the project developments provided useful capabilities.

Boeing said in a statement it was pleased the Department of Homeland Security planned to continue using surveillance towers already constructed and that it "remain committed to providing valuable solutions and supporting DHS."

'FAR WISER APPROACH'

An assessment of the Boeing program released by DHS found that $1 billion was spent to cover just 53 miles in Arizona. The new approach should cost less than $750 million to cover the rest of Arizona's border, some 323 miles, DHS said.

"The department's decision to use technology based on the particular security needs of each segment of the border is a far wiser approach, and I hope it will be more cost effective," said Senate Homeland Security Committee Chairman Joe Lieberman.

While other lawmakers also hailed the end to SBInet, the Republican chairman of the House Homeland Security Committee expressed concern there would be further delays in beefing up security along the border.

"The Obama administration must promptly present the people of this country with a comprehensive plan to secure our borders, incorporating the necessary staffing, fencing, and technology," said Representative Peter King.

The market for hi-tech border solutions is worth billions of dollars and the competition is fierce.

Other firms in the market include defense and homeland security contractor Raytheon and Arizona-based ICx Technologies, which develop and market high-tech detection and surveillance systems with border security uses.

"There were things that (SBInet) did right, and things that it did wrong, but one of the concerns was always that this was more of a gimmick than substance. By pulling it, that tends to reinforce that impression," said Steven Camarota, research director of the Center for Immigration Studies think tank.

The Boeing project had been on the chopping block for some time. Napolitano last year pulled $50 million of funding for it that was included in the economic stimulus package and she froze other funds for it pending a review.

She said in March the money would be used instead to buy existing technologies such as thermal imaging devices and ultra-light plane detection systems.

We don't need a "virtual fence". We need an actual fence, with actual soldiers - that have actual guns and actual bullets.

The United States is faced with a 9.4% unemployment rate and the President and Secretary of the Department of Homeland Security can not understand that by building a real fence we can create thousands of jobs for the unemployed and make a major improvement in the flow of illegals coming across the southern border. There has to be some underlying motive for the President and the rest of the Democratic administration for not wanting to secure our borders? Could it be that they are planning some back door and underhand policy to start granting amnesty? Look at all the votes the Democrats could gain by the amnesty program. Everyone knows that over 70% of the Hispanics vote for the Democrats and their entitlement programs.

Personally I don't care how much money as a taxpayer I have to pay to put up a border fence. It is nothing compared to the billions of dollars dished out every year for the illegals with their anchor babies, welfare, food stamps, section 8 housing, paying no taxes, having no or stolen social security numbers. It is nothing compared to that amount of money. Close the borders. Come over her legally if you can.

ILLEGALS THAT ARE IN THE UNITED STATES:

We need to make sure that they are all deported. Our economic system does not have the resources to keep paying entitlements to these people. It they want to live in our country they need to understand that we have immigration laws that are to be followed. Now all we have to do is contact each of our representatives and make sure that they understand that the people want our laws enforced.

The Constitution of the United States of America is a fluid document that is interpreted in light of prevailing customs and norms. 200+ years ago, what might have been acceptable criminal punishment is now deemed cruel and inhumane. Similarly, 200+ years ago, or indeed up until the 1920s, virtually anyone could immigrate to the United States. The times have changed and we have strong laws on our books. When the federal government chooses not to enforce each and every law for one group of people but not others, and that has an adverse impact on United States citizens' property and safety, states should be able to craft supplemental but non-conflicting legislation to protect its citizens. In every poll out there on the Arizona law, a minimum of 66% of United States citizens agree. This is not a race issue. If there were 20 million illegal Europeans in the United States they would need to go as well.

I wonder why there is so much commotion being made about airport security? I find it offensive to think that someone is going to pat me down if I choose to fly. They can use the detection devices that are at all airports and forget about imposing on individuals private parts in a pat down. The airport security systems have been used by the government to indicate that they are concerned about terrorists entering the United States. That is great but we can overdue the checking procedure.

Now let's get to the real problem that the United States should be worried about. It is just amazing that the Department of Homeland Security, the Justice Department, President Obama, Senator Reid, Nancy Pelosi and Eric Holder can not see or understand that our borders are not protected in any manner. When a state tries to implement a program to ease the threat the President and his lemmings start legal proceedings against the state. There are about 1 million illegals that enter into the United States every year through our southern borders. I would hate to know how many terrorists are among those that are walking freely into our country. Until the government becomes aware of the need for complete border security it seems rather foolish to worry about the airport security to the extreme. There is nothing happening along the southern border that will prevent terrorists from coming into the United States.

The major affect that the illegals have in America is to try and destroy our standard of living and turn our beautiful country into another third world country that does not seem to care whether it is kept clean and respectful. How dare they come into our country and demand the same rights as the American citizens and the legal immigrants. Americans work very hard to preserve our freedoms and protect our rights. We do not appreciate the fact that the illegals grab the Mexican flag and do protest marches against our country because we do not want to make them citizens.

There are thousands of illegals marching through our southern border every week. They do not have any fear of the border patrol and leave miles of garbage strewn all over the Arizona Desert. It is outrageous that our federal government does not enforce the laws of our country. We need to contact every representative and make sure that they vote to stop amnesty and finish the construction of the border fence. There can not be any amnesty if we want America to return to "America the Beautiful"

This is the problem with most of the illegals. They do not want to become citizens of the United States of America. They do not want to adapt to the ways of our country. They do not want to respect the flag of the United Starts. They want all of our benefits and entitlement programs but do not want to give up their heritage. There is no such thing as Mexican Americans. If they want to be Mexican then they can go back to Mexico.

If they want to live here they need to be Americans. There can not be any form of amnesty for any illegal that is in the United States of America.

When we complete building the border fence and secure the entry into the United States will eliminate over 1 million illegals from entering our country every year. This will be a major contributing factor to solving our deficit and unemployment problems. When will the United States Congress and the President wake up and do so something about the problem? Stop our representatives from pampering the Hispanic vote and start looking out for the American vote.

JUAREZ IS A DYING CITY - AMERICAN CITIES COULD BE NEXT IF WE DO NOT SECURE OUR BORDERS. DON'T FOOL YOURSELF THE CARTELS ARE NOT AGAINST DOING THE SAME THING IN AMERICA.

By WILL WEISSERT, Associated Press Will Weissert, Associated Press – Wed Dec 29, 4:39 pm ET

CIUDAD JUAREZ, Mexico – The mother of four raised a finger, pointing out abandoned and stripped concrete homes and counting how many families have fled the Western Hemisphere's deadliest city on her street alone.

"One, two, three, four, here, and two more back there on the next block," said Laura Longoria.

The 36-year-old ran a convenience store in her working-class neighborhood in south Juarez until the owner's closed shop, fed up with the tribute they were forced to pay to drug gangsters to stay in business.

Her family vowed to stick it out. But then came the kidnapping of a teen from a stationery shop across the street. After that, Longoria's husband, Enrique Mondragon, requested a transfer from the bus company where he works.

"They asked, 'where to,'" he recalled. "I said, 'Anywhere.'"

No one knows how many residents have left the city of 1.4 million since a turf battle over border drug corridors unleashed an unprecedented wave of cartel murders and mayhem. Business leaders, citing government tax information, say the exodus could number 110,000, while a municipal group and local university say that it's closer to 230,000 and estimates by social organizations are even higher.

The tally is especially hard to track because Juarez is by nature transitory, attracting thousands of workers to high-turnover jobs in manufacturing, or who use the city across the Rio Grande from El Paso, Texas, as a way station before they slip north illegally.

But its toll is everywhere you look. Barely a week goes by when Longoria and her husband don't watch a neighbor move away. Then the vandals arrive, carrying off window panes, pipes, even light fixtures, until there's nothing but a graffiti-covered shell, surrounded by yards strewn with rotting food or shredded tires. That could be what's in store for Longoria's three-room home of poured concrete if her husband's transfer comes through.

Long controlled by the Juarez Cartel, the city descended into a horrifying cycle of violence after Mexico's most-wanted kingpin, Joaquin "El Chapo" Guzman, and his Sinaloa Cartel tried to shoot their way to power here beginning in 2008. President Felipe Calderon sent nearly 10,000 troops to restore order. Now, the Mexican army and federal authorities are going door-to-door, conducting an emergency census to determine just how many residents have fled.

Many people, however, refuse to answer their questions for fear authorities are simply collecting information about neighborhoods so they can begin extorting residents — just like the drug gangs. "Soon," Longoria said, "there won't be many people left to count."

While many Juarez residents fleeing the violence seek out more peaceful points in Mexico, others have streamed across the border into El Paso, population 740,000, where apartment vacancies are down and requests for new utility services in recently purchased or rented houses have spiked, according to Mayor John Cook.

Massacres, beheadings, YouTube videos featuring cartel torture sessions and even car bombs are becoming commonplace in Juarez, where more than 3,300 people have been killed this year, according to the federal government, making it among the most dangerous places on earth.

El Paso, by contrast, has had three violent deaths — and one was a murder-suicide.

Juarez Chamber of Commerce President Daniel Murguia said at least 6,000 city businesses have closed so far this year, according to Mexican Interior Ministry figures. There is no data available on those shuttered amid last year's and 2008 violence, however, or on scores of businesses targeted by arsonists.

Kathy Dodson, El Paso's economic director, said the number of fees paid for new city business permits there have not increased dramatically, but Jose Luis Mauricio, president of a group for new Mexican business owners in El Paso known as "La Red," or The Net, said membership has grown from nine in February to about 280 today.

"Maybe it's a bit sad for Juarez, but these are business owners who are moving here because they have no choice," said Mauricio, who leads weekly breakfasts for Mexican expatriates looking to set up businesses in El Paso.

One club member is a Mexican-American who owns a factory in Juarez but moved to El Paso with his family after he was kidnapped last year. The 50-year-old, who asked that his name not be published to avoid further repercussions, was held in a Juarez safe house — but managed to untie his hands and cry for help loud enough that neighbors called the Mexican army to rescue him.

"There's a lot of people afraid. I don't blame them. Even if they haven't had a bad experience, they don't want to be the next one to have one, so they run away," said the factory owner. He said he will never move back to Juarez but hopes the violence will one day calm enough for him to visit.

"It's a city that's dying," he said. "It's out of control."

Many of those who have not left want to, including Marta Elena Ramirez.

She owns Restaurant Dona Chole, specializing in menudo, a clear soup made with beef stomach. Her cafeteria-style eatery is on the second floor of an indoor market of Mexican handicrafts.

Ramirez said sales are down 50 percent since 2007, when Americans used to head south for drinking and clubbing, or to stock up on Mexican knicknacks. Now they are too afraid to come.

Though she has held U.S. residency for 18 years, Ramirez lives in Juarez and had never considered moving — until now. She's stopped paying rent on her restaurant and is looking for investors to help her start a street food cart in El Paso.

"I've always been a fighter, and this is my Juarez. I've always said, `No matter what happens, Juarez is mine,'" said the 65-year-old. "But too much has happened."

As commerce in the city dries up, even Juarez residents who do not move north cross into El Paso more frequently for services no longer available in their neighborhoods and spend $220 million a year in El Paso, said Murguia.

"Here it's a problem of opportunity, not just violence," he said. "There are no jobs, and that means there are more people who are becoming hit men and criminals."

Even for those not tied to drug trafficking, staying in Juarez means paying off extortionists — like a 43-year-old food wholesaler near the city's center who provides everything from bulk dog food to beer that smaller stores use to stock their shelves.

In September 2009, associates from "La Linea," enforcers for the Juarez Cartel comprised of hit men and corrupt police and soldiers, visited his store and said he would be required to pay 4,000 pesos — about $330 — a week "for protection."

"They came to see me in a very friendly way," said the business owner, who asked that his name and key details be omitted so he could not be identified. "Everyone is paying. Those who aren't paying are out of business, even dead."

As recently as 2008, he had 500 wholesale customers; now it's down to 200. Two storeowners who used to do business with him have been gunned down in their stores over the last year, and a third shot dead in his kitchen. Business got so slow that his extortionists recently reduced his weekly payment to 2,500 pesos, about $205, but warned him never to miss a week.

Every week, the wholesaler receives a call in which a distorted voice provides a bank account number where money can be deposited but not withdrawn. He takes cash to indicated bank branches and makes deposits.

The wholesaler's son-in-law was kidnapped early last year — the family put $230,000 on a debit card and exchanged it for his safe return. His store had also been burglarized previously. Since he began paying for protection, however, all crime around him has ceased and his customers have even stopped getting harassed by police for illegally parking in front of his business.

"At first, I used to say 'this will pass,' but now I'm resigned that there's no solution," said the wholesaler, who has applied for U.S. residency to move to El Paso.

Murguia said extortion payments are now so common that they've become known as "cobras del piso" or "floor charges" for doing business in Juarez — but that there's no measure of how much payoffs cost business citywide per year because few admit to paying them.

Many familiar Juarez restaurants have shut down only to pop up anew on the U.S. side. The high-end Mexican eatery Maria Chuhchena closed its original location in Juarez and resurfaced in El Paso, though the restaurant maintains a branch in Juarez's spiffy Campestre district. Another Juarez favorite, Aroma, was one of three eateries set ablaze by arsonists on a single night in June 2008 and now operates in El Paso.

Now parts of Juarez after sundown are all but deserted — even in the heart of downtown. Closed used car dealerships, taco and hamburger stands, pharmacies, ice cream parlors and muffler shops give way to a block of abandoned doctors' and dentists' offices, which stand forlornly next to a closed stereo outlet and across from an empty office supply store.

"Se renta" and "se vende," signs offering retail space for rent or sale are everywhere, plastered to the shuttered pizzeria, the closed and looted furniture store, the defunct locksmith and the empty facade of "Jersey Mechanic."

Other abandoned properties are tagged with a simple phrase in black spray paint: "How many more?"

We are going to present some information about what is happening in the United States right now. These statistics were from the Department of Homeland Security or the Federal Bureau of Investigation. These statistics are from the same people that are advocating amnesty to the illegals. These are real statistics and not some fringe group statistics. With all the negative reports being printed/broadcast in the liberal progressive news media (New York Times, CBS, NBC ABC, MSNBC, CNN, etc) here are the statistics they don't deem news worthy and fail to report. This is really sad –

- 83% of warrants for murder in Phoenix are for illegal aliens.

- 86% of warrants for murder in Albuquerque are for illegal aliens.

- 75% of those on the most wanted list in Los Angeles, Phoenix and Albuquerque are illegal aliens.

- 24.9% of all inmates in California detention centers are Mexican nationals.

- 40.1% of all inmates in Arizona detention centers are Mexican nationals.

- 48.2% of all inmates in New Mexico detention centers are Mexican nationals.

- 29% (630,000) convicted illegal alien felons fill our State and Federal prisons at a cost of $1.6 billion annually.

- 53% plus of all investigated burglaries reported in California, New Mexico, Nevada, Arizona and Texas are perpetrated by illegal aliens.

- 50% plus of all gang members in Los Angeles are illegal aliens.

- 71% plus of all apprehended cars stolen in 2005 in Texas, New Mexico, Arizona, Nevada and California were stolen by Illegal aliens or "transport coyotes".

- 47% of cited/stopped drivers in California have no license, no insurance and no registration for the vehicle. Of that 47%, 92% are illegal aliens.

- 63% of cited/stopped drivers in Arizona have no license, no insurance and no registration for the vehicle. Of that 63%, 97% are illegal aliens.

- 66% of cited/stopped drivers in New Mexico have no license, no insurance and no registration for the vehicle. Of that 66% 98% are illegal aliens.

- 380,000 plus "anchor babies" were born in the US to illegal alien parents in just one year, making 380,000 babies automatically US citizens which should be unconstitutional.

- 97.2% of all costs incurred from those illegal births were paid by the American taxpayers.

And remember YOU are supporting ALL of these illegal migrants no matter where they are now. Every time another illegal runs the border breaking our laws, your pocket just gets lighter and robbed more.

How can any branch of the United States government even think about giving this type of person amnesty to become an American citizen? That is absurd.

As reported by Newsmax on September 18, 2010, there is another Arizona sheriff that believes the Obama administration is undermining the rule of law on the border by blocking the border enforcement needed to prevent illegals and narco terrorists from flooding into the United States from Mexico. Pinal County Sheriff Paul Babeu stated that the administration has actively thwarted law enforcement efforts to help secure the border. Now why does that not surprise anyone? The Mexican drug cartels now control some parts of the Arizona border. Currently there are militant groups who are escorting drug carriers or human illegals with AK-47's. They are much more organized than the American public is aware of. They have lookout points on the miles of Arizona border and know when the border patrols are going to be in the area and when they will have free access to enter into the United States.

The Obama administration has sued the state of Arizona for enforcing the current laws and wants to leap frog over border security and just go right to amnesty. We can not let such a disgrace to the American people happen. The border fence needs to be completed now. We could build the fence and reduce unemployment by hiring thousands to complete this project immediately. Put the United States Army Corps of Engineering in charge to supervise the labor force and get the job done. It could be a project similar to the Hoover Dam. Thousands of workers were hired from all over the United States to complete that project.

A Federal Bureau of Investigation statistic shows that violent crime went down in the San Diego, California area by 52% in the year following the completion of that section of the border wall. What are we waiting for?

This is the only symbol of the American pride and our flag. It has to be the only flag flown in the United States.

PROGRAM TWO:

THE EFFECTS OF IMMIGRATION:

The primary requirements for obtaining a United States citizenship are dependent on total allegiance to America, not mere physical geography. The purpose of this model legislation is to restore the original intent of the 14th Amendment, which is currently being misapplied and is encouraging illegal aliens to cross and cost American taxpayers $113 billion annually, or nearly $1,117 yearly per individual taxpayer.

When you read the following you will understand why California is broke and will not do anything to fix the problem.

Phoenix, AZ (AP) - SB-1070 is having an effect.

Illegal immigrants are boycotting Arizona by the thousands, showing their outrage with Arizona's controversial new SB-1070 law by moving elsewhere.

In the small town of Guadalupe AZ, south of Phoenix, Manuel Renaldo is one of those who are punishing Arizona by leaving.

As he loaded his stolen car with his belongings and family of ten, Renaldo told this reporter through an interpreter

"It's a matter of principle. I refuse to be supported by a state that treats me like a criminal."

The effects of the exodus are being felt by Arizona retailers who are reporting dwindling sales of beer, spray paint, and ammunition. Also hit hard are the state's hospitals, which have reported a dramatic decline in births and emergency room visits. Tattoo parlors are in a state of panic.

Renaldo told a reporter through an interpreter "He and his family are moving to California, which is a state that will support him and his family with dignity."

You have to love Arizona. It is too bad that the other states are not trying to solve the illegal problem.

HOW IMMIGRATION AFFECTS POPULATON:

In 1900, the United States population was 76 million and there were an estimated 500,000 Hispanics. The Census Bureau projects that by 2050, 28% of the population will be of Hispanic descent. This demographic shift is largely fueled by immigration from Latin America. These figures do not include the 20,000,000 illegals that are in the United States.

When you add in the number of babies that these produce the numbers will increase by 100 million people by the year 2050. How do the politicians expect the United States to support all of these people?

The Census Bureau estimates the United States population will grow from 281 million in 2000 to 397 million in 2050 with immigration, but only to 328 million with no immigration. A new report from the Pew Research Center projects that by 2050, non-Hispanic whites will account for 47% of the population, down from the 2005 figure of 67%. Non-Hispanic whites made up 85% of the population in 1960. It also foresees the Hispanic population rising from 14% in 2005 to 29% by 2050. The Asian population is expected to more than triple by 2050. Overall, the population of the United States is due to rise from 296 million in 2005 to 438 million in 2050, with 82% of the increase from immigrants.

These numbers are without the illegals in the United States.

Further studies have indicated that 70% of the largest cities in the United States show that American Caucasians at the last census are predicted to be in the minority. In California American Caucasians slipped from 80% of the population in 1970 to 42.3% of the states population in 2008. It has also gotten worse in the last three years.

Studies have shown that 31% of adult immigrants have not completed high school. A third lack health insurance. Poor immigrants strain public services such as local schools and health care. From 2000 to 2006, 41 percent of the increase in people without health insurance occurred among Hispanics. According to the immigration reduction advocacy group Center for Immigration Studies, 25.8% of Mexican immigrants live in poverty, which is more than double the rate for natives in 1999. Another report shows that from 1990 to 2006, the number of poor Hispanics increased by 3.2 million, from 6 million to 9.2 million.

We do not have to search very far for the answer as to why the Democrats seek to provide amnesty for these illegals. History indicates that over 68% of the Hispanic voters are Democratic.

In a 2002 study, which took place soon after the September 11 attacks, 55% of Americans favored decreasing legal immigration, 27% favored keeping it at the same level, and 15% favored increasing it. In 2006, the immigration reduction advocacy think tank the Center for Immigration Studies released a poll that found that 68% of Americans think the United States immigration levels are too high, and just 2% said they are too low. They also found that 70% said they would vote for candidates that are in favor of decreasing legal immigration.

When polls are taken regarding the illegals that have entered into the United States the citizens are 70% in favor of deporting them and closing our borders to stop the flow coming into the United States.

Illegal Immigration Reform and Immigrant Responsibility Act of 1996:

The Illegal Immigration Reform and Immigrant Responsibility Act of 1996, Public. Law 104-208, Division C, 110 Statute 3009-546 vastly changed the immigration laws of the United States. In 1996 the Illegal Immigration Reform and Immigrant Responsibility Act (IIRAIRA 96) was passed and signed by President Bill Clinton. Title III of this new act created the notion of "unlawfully present" persons; specifically, the three-year, ten-year, and permanent bars were formed.

This act states that if an immigrant has been unlawfully present in the United States for 180 days but less than 365 days he or she must remain outside the United States for three years unless the person obtains a pardon. If the person has been in the United States for 365 days or more, he or she must stay outside the United States for ten years unless he or she obtains a pardon. If the person returns to the United States without the pardon, the person cannot apply for a waiver for a period of ten years. This is the permanent bar.

Constitutional issues within the law:

Previously, immediate deportation was triggered only for offenses that could lead to five years or more in jail. Under the Act, minor offenses such as shoplifting, may make an individual eligible for deportation. When IIRIRA was passed in 1996, it was applied retroactively to all those convicted of deportable offenses. However, in 2001, the United States Supreme Court decided that Congress did not intend IIRIRA to be applied retroactively to those who pleaded guilty to a crime prior to the enactment of IIRIRA, if that person would not have been deportable at the time that he pleaded guilty. IIRIRA's mandatory detention provisions have also been repeatedly challenged, with less success.

Deportation issues:

Deportees may be held in jail for months, even as much as two years, before being brought before an immigration board, at which defendants need to pay for their own legal representation. In 2001, the Supreme Court curtailed the Immigration Service's ability to hold deportees indefinitely.

Section 287(g) and relations between federal and lower levels of government;

IIRIRA addressed the relationship between the federal government and local governments. Section 287(g) is a program of the act that permits the Secretary of the Department of Homeland Security to enter into agreements with state and local law enforcement agencies, permitting designated officers to perform immigration law enforcement functions, pursuant to a Memorandum of Agreement. This section does not simply deputize state and local law enforcement personnel to enforce immigration matters. This provision was implemented by local and state authorities in five states, California, Arizona, Alabama, Florida and North Carolina by the end of 2006.

The question really is how come the Department of Homeland Security, the President, the Attorney General and the Congress do not enforce the laws that are on the books? We need to elect the representatives in government that will enforce the laws of the country instead of taking legal action against the state of Arizona that wants to follow the law. Contact your representatives now and make sure that they will start following all of the laws. America can not afford to allow a million illegals to enter our country every year. We need to deport all of them immediately.

HOW ILLEGALS AFFECT THE UNITED STATES:

14 states may target birthright citizenship

By Liz Goodwin

Arizona state politicians will introduce model legislation this week to encourage states to prevent children of illegal immigrants from being granted citizenship under the 14th Amendment. Lawmakers in at least 14 states have said they are committed to passing the legislation targeting birthright citizenship. Arizona's anti-illegal-immigrant bill, SB-1070, was also based on model legislation that could be easily copied by states, and at least seven states are likely to pass bills similar to the first Arizona immigration overhaul this year, according to one analysis by an immigrants rights group.

Arizona state Senator Russell Pearce will unveil the bill Jan. 5 in Washington, D.C., the Arizona Capital Times reports. The paper says lawmakers in Alabama, Arizona, Delaware, Idaho, Indiana, Michigan, Mississippi, Montana, Nebraska, New Hampshire, Oklahoma, Pennsylvania, Texas and Utah have said they want to introduce similar legislation this year.

Pearce argues that the "original intent" of the 14th Amendment was to grant citizenship to freed United States slaves, and that it was never meant to apply to the children of foreigners. A Phoenix New Times writer, however, argues that lawmakers who originally passed the amendment took into account the cases of children of Chinese immigrants in California as well as children of gypsies when drafting the measure. A 19th-century Supreme Court precedent also backs that interpretation, though no Supreme Court case has yet dealt with the issue of offspring of illegal immigrant parents.

The amendment states: "All persons born or naturalized in the United States, and subject to the jurisdiction thereof, are citizens of the United States and of the State wherein they reside."

Ali Noorani of the immigrant-rights group the National Immigration Forum told The Lookout that he believes leaders in more states will try to counter the thrust of the birthright initiative by adopting resolutions that eschew state laws cracking down on illegal immigration. Religious and political leaders in Utah recently signed a compact advocating for a "humane" approach to immigration, which other states could copy.

After reading the feedback from the supporters of the American Citizens Political Action Committee we are firmly convinced that the United States of American need to enforce the following policies with regard to securing our southern borders. The members and supporters of the American Citizens PAC are in favor of supporting candidates that will vote for the following:

- **Complete the Southern Border fence as quickly as possible.**

- **Pass legislation to have our military personnel control the Southern Border until the border fence is completed.**

- **Pass legislation that will repeal of the 14th amendment to the Constitution of the United States.**

- **Pass legislation that will fine all landlords that rent to illegals and all the employers that hire illegals.**

- **Do not pass any legislation that will provide amnesty for anyone including their anchor babies.**

- **Deport all of the illegals that are in the United States.**

The following comments are from supporters of the American Citizens Political Action Committee. They indicate that the people are tired of what is happening in Washington and are ready to insist that our representatives start listening to the people.

It is about time that the US government addressed the 14th amendment for the purpose it was truly intended for and not what the Libtards would like to spin it into. It is not about ANY child born of an illegal family, but about Slaves and their children.

We need to send ALL ILLEGALS out of this country! They can take their offspring with them they are not citizens here

I have lived in the States all my life and they have more rights and freedoms than I have. It's high time they go back to their own country or start the procedures to become legal.

No other country grants citizenship to the children of illegal aliens. Other countries put the illegal immigrants in jail. It's time to end this.

It's a load of crap that children of those here ILLEGALLY, who have already BROKEN our laws are granted citizenship! Why do we reward criminals? There is no way the people who passed the 14th Amendment would have approved of this wholesale invasion by a foreign country. Stop the insanity.

we need to worry about the citizens we have already instead of these boarder jumpers and their babies. All of which are draining the economy and using public aid meant to help Americans not illegals.

It's a magnet for pregnant illegals and as a result two hospitals on central coast of California shut down-I know, I lived there + had friends in administration. Who do you think pays for their deliveries, then healthcare for children + mother, then schooling, etc., etc..

The Mexicans have abused everything they can touch in this country. They need to stay home and fix the problems they have instead of running here with their hands out, I hope this passes and forces the government to look at the will of the people, we fear that brown tide that consume us all if they don't act to stop it

This wouldn't be necessary if the federal government did their job and protected the border. Remember when they went after Arizona, saying "It isn't up to states to decide immigration laws"? Then why did they not go after sanctuary cities and cities that refuse to enforce immigration laws? If you actually enforced the laws and protected the border to begin with, we wouldn't have to deal with all this crap now. Seal and protect the border, THEN worry about fixing immigration. All you are doing is treating the symptoms and not the actual problem.

If the parents are here illegally then the children are also here illegally and should not have birth right citizenship. All these people are doing is abusing the 14th Amendment and other laws in the U.S. It has to start and stop somewhere and this is a good place to start.

So... does Mexico offer citizenship to the infant child of a foreigner...NO

Actually, No other country offers birthright citizenship. These illegals cross the border with the sole purpose of delivering their child on U.S. soil so as to be able to reap the benefits of our social welfare system. They come here and become a burden on our society and cause me to pay higher taxes.

Citizenship should be granted to children of citizens and those who immigrated legally...period.

I'm a 30 year veteran and I say 'finish the fence' and get these laws passed now.

I have no problems at all with legal immigrants at all but the law to give automatic citizenship to children was never meant for millions of illegal aliens that come here and for citizens of other countries that fly here just to have their child and then go back home a week later to their country with a child that is a U.S. citizen.

I work in State Government and see this crap all day long. Illegal from Mexico gets Illegal from Nicaragua pregnant = baby born in USA and now all 3 on Government tab. Also I have personally caught Illegals with fraudulent documents-- they are arrested, then released, I go to court at their hearing and they don't show up = warrant issued but they are only arrested if they get stopped on a traffic violation and warrant shows up. I asked why they don't go to their place of business or home and arrest them and told we don't have the manpower. It also burns me up that we have all these Refugees and Parolees in this country on Government assistance. Who the hell invited them? I know sure as hell I didn't.

One way to slow the flow of the illegals from wanting to enter the United States illegally would be to place an excise tax on any funds that are wired from the United States to Mexico or any other foreign country. It is estimated that there are between $25 billion to $40 billion wired into Mexico every year. Placing an excise tax of 25% would provide a nice amount of money that could be used to complete our southern border fence. Let them pay for the problem that they are causing.

Another fact that will affect the number of illegals in the United States would be to place severe fines and jail time to any landlord that rents or sells property to an illegal. That would include groups of illegals joining together with one legal immigrant so they can place several families in one unit. Then make sure that any one that hires an illegal be fined an amount that will make it impossible to make any money hiring illegals. That fine should be in the range of $20,000 to $50,000 per violation. Any employer that has more than 5 violations will face mandatory jail time of 30 days for each illegal hired.

When you take away any chance of having employment or a place to live you will see a voluntary flow of illegals back to where they came from and the program will not cost the government one dime.

Time for this to be a national law. We can no longer afford to grant citizenship to anyone who runs across the border once their water breaks and now their kids are US citizens. We can't even take care of our own, why do we need to take care of everyone else?

Illegal mothers come here expressly to have the baby knowing that the baby will anchor her and the future family waiting in Mexico. This idiocy must stop.

When the senate failed to pass the Dream Act on 18 Dec, Jorje-Mario Cabera, a spokesman for the Coalition for humane Immigrant Rights in LA said, "This is a dark day in America." Get over it amigo. We need to start rounding up and deporting all illegal aliens. Sheriff Joe is ready.

The 14th amendment was written to protect slaves, and since illegal occupation wasn't an issue then, there is no way that the framers of this amendment was trying to protect the children of illegal immigrants, and it therefore does not apply to anchor babies.

Really, this is about anchor babies. "My child i' American, so my familia get to stay here and ra' him." No way. Finger print the kid and then tell the family the kid can stay or return when he's 18, but THEY have to go back to their country of origin. I have zero sympathy for people who knowingly break the law then expect it to protect them from punishment. I have zero respect for any American who would want illegals to come here and use their vote to persuade politicians to overlook them.

No matter the original intent of the 14th, citizens now clearly want change, and as a Democracy for the people by the people our elected officials have a duty to act upon the wants of the majority. Clearly our wants are changing as should our "Amendments"

I believe that at this current time we need to declare a moratorium on legal immigration for at least 5 years. Also, we need to stop and reverse all illegal immigration. The immigration today is destroying our Western culture-- our ideals, traditions, language, customs, laws, economic system, etc. The

American people never voted directly FOR this. If we were given a chance, we would have voted AGAINST this. The immigrants of today need to be told that they must assimilate into our country and learn our language. We should not be forced to assimilate to their ways. Also, we must realize that we do not need to accept everyone into this country that applies for citizenship. With the high unemployment that we have, allowing more and more immigrants and aliens to move into our country will continue to create higher unemployment in the years to come.

Kick them and their kids out nothing but a drain in the USA... we pay and pay while they sit and get things for free... while we have to pay out the butt for things... they get free housing and food and education and we cant even send our kids to college.. Americans should be able to go to school for free. While we pay for their education. This is so wrong I am for sending all of them back where they belong and closing off the boarders and making sure everyone who is here have an ID and papers on hand at all times. I am for profiling. If they have papers they should have nothing to worry about. Press one for ENGLISH My butt. More like if you cant speak English.... LEARN TO SPEAK IT........or get out

Why have immigration laws, if we are never going to enforce them? If you sneak in the country, you are illegal, and your kids are not citizens.

To make citizens of kids whose parents broke our laws, would open the flood gates of millions of pregnant mothers who would more than happily sneak in, become a citizen, then immediately run down to the local welfare office.

Americium tax payers, are heavily burdened as it is, with billions of dollars having to be spent on social services, and incarceration for illegals.

Come in legally, just as millions of others have. There's no easy answer for this problem of Illegal Immigration. Most of these people are poor and are trying to start a better life. On the other hand most come to this country for the Welfare, and state provided assistance programs. Most don't want to give up being Mexican but they want all of the benefits of being American. I am sure that most of the listed states above are sick of Illegals running free on American soil.....So, whets the solution then?

Listed below are several of the arguments that have been used by misguided people to try and justify illegal immigration. Next to each is the reason why each of these arguments has no merit.

1) They are an economic necessity - Not true. The idea that a bunch of desperately poor, uneducated, unskilled, illegal foreigners are an economic necessity is ludicrous. In fact, when you compare cost vs. benefit, it is obvious that they are not only NOT a necessity, they are not even an asset. Rather, they are a liability and a huge one at that.

2) They do work Americans won't do - Not true. They do work Americans won't do for $5 an hour (especially if Americans can collect welfare and unemployment forever). Of course, if you got rid of the illegals, the jobs wouldn't pay $5 an hour. The people who wanted the work done would have to pay a wage that was attractive enough to get Americans to do the work. And it might even be enough so Americans could support themselves and get off welfare and unemployment.

3) They work & contribute to our society - So do I. And if I break the law and commit crimes, I can expect to pay a penalty of some kind it could range from a small fine to the death penalty. I do not get rewarded. This argument makes no sense.

4) They are just trying to make better lives - Aren't we all? The difference is that most of us understand that we don't have a right to acquire by illegal means those things that we find difficult to acquire by legal means. And we certainly don't have the right to do it in a foreign country. Mexico does not allow foreigners to enter their country illegally and break its laws. If you believe differently, go give it a try. Call me collect from the dungeon. Let me know how it went.

5) It is impossible to round up and deport the illegals - We don't have to. All we have to do is remove the incentives that brought them here in the first place. No jobs. No housing. No services. No benefits. Once we remove the incentives that brought them here, they will leave on their own.

6) It would be too expensive to round them up and deport them - See #5.

7) Immigration control is racist - This is just another play of the race card by people who have no other cards to play. Immigration control is the world-wide status quo. There is nothing racist about it. Furthermore, the USA welcomes LEGAL immigrants of all races and ethnicities from all over the world who have gone through the legal immigration process. This is not just a bad argument; it is an attempt to create hatred and division.

8) We are a nation of immigrants - We are a nation that has, historically, allowed and even encouraged legal immigration. And we continue to do so. The issue at hand is illegal immigration, which has nothing to do with legal immigration. This argument is totally irrelevant.

9) They are people. We must treat them humanely - Yes & yes. But let's not pretend like they are victims who were dragged here kicking and screaming against their will. Nothing could be further from the truth. They came of their own free will and for their own benefit and they broke the law to do it. People should not be rewarded for breaking laws and committing crimes. Sending them home is the right thing to do. There is nothing "draconian" about it.

No other country on Earth allows foreigners to come in illegally, work illegally, steal jobs from its citizens, break laws, commit crimes (serious crimes!), evade taxes, etc. etc. etc. And there are no rational reasons why we should either. There are only political reasons, and they aren't rational.

I just laugh at anyone who brings up the fact Mexico owned Texas and it was "stolen", blah, blah, blah. Ah, well who owned it before the Mexicans? (Spanish) Don't they have the real claim to it? The entire Southwest became developed and rich because of being part of the United States. If you think we took it - we did that to every State in the Union for goodness sakes. As long as we stay strong we can keep it/all of them too. If the Mexicans want to try and take it back, bring it on. They only want it now because of what hard working Americans have done for 165 years to develop it. Now that it is worth something. Get to work in Mexico and see what you can do on your own - quit being parasites, and quit poking the dog before you get bit - real hard.

Every dollar that goes to an illegal is one less for Americans who worked their whole life building this country, one less dollar to go to your parents or grand parents care, your child's education, the disabled and veterans! Wonder why they did not receive a COLA increase the last 2 years?

We need to do this and put every business owner in prison for 30 years "no loop holes to get out" that hire illegal aliens and they will stop coming because they cant get hired anywhere and when they go to the hospital to give birth to children send them back to Mexico and send the country of Mexico the bill for the hospital they are putting a huge burden on our schools, hospitals and economy its got to stop

Unfortunately, we have a President, Attorney General, Secretary of Homeland Security and Congress that does not want to offend the Hispanic voters. These politicians do not care if they offend the citizens of America.

Every American should be contacting their representatives at all levels of government and demanding that they endorse defending our borders and deporting all illegals that are in the country today and for the rest of time. Secure our borders and stop the flow by placing our military personnel on duty at the border. Why do we defend the borders of other countries and forget about our own?

THE PROBLEM ALL STARTS HERE

PROGRAM THREE:

THE FEDERAL DEFICIT:

Battle Brewing Over Federal Debt Limit

As a new and politically divided Congress convened the newly elected majority of Republicans and the White House seem to be on a collision course over whether to raise the federal debt ceiling.

Some Republican lawmakers have vowed not to vote to raise the debt limit unless there is a plan in place for dealing with long-term obligations, including Social Security, and for returning to 2008 spending levels.

But the White House says that refusing to raise the limit would have a "catastrophic" impact on the economy. "That would be a worse financial economic crisis than anything we saw in 2008," White House economist Austan Goolsbee said. A critical showdown could come as early as March with the debt ceiling at $14.294 trillion and the debt at nearly $14 trillion and growing daily.

The tax cut package that President Obama and Republican leaders negotiated at the end of last year pushed the government about three weeks closer to the debt limit, an official told Fox Business.

Republicans have vowed to shrink government and ease federal oversight of the private sector as part of their solution to heal a damaged economy. They have pledged to vote on bills that cut spending at least once a week.

The first spending cut vote is set for Thursday, a 5 percent reduction in the amount ticketed for lawmakers' and committees' offices as well as leadership staff. Aides estimated the savings at $35 million over the next nine months.

But Social Security, Medicare and defense spending account for a lion's share of the federal budget.

Incoming Majority Leader Eric Cantor of Virginia left the door open to potential defense cuts in a remarkable change of policy.

"Everything is going to be on the table," Cantor said. In the Pledge with America, Republicans called for across-the-board cuts in nondiscretionary spending. But they said that defense and homeland security funding would not be touched.

Obama has expressed confidence that he will be able to work with Republicans who will control the House and an additional five seats in the Senate.

"I'm pretty confident that they're going to recognize that our job is to govern and make sure that we are delivering jobs for the American people and that we are creating a competitive economy for the 21st century," Obama said on Tuesday on his return flight from a two-week holiday in Hawaii.

THE UNITED STATES DEBT CEILING:

Presidents have no Constitutional authority to levy taxes or spend money, as this responsibility resides with the Congress, although a President's priorities influence Congressional action. The Congress was controlled by the Democrats from January 2007 and should be held accountable for the massive increase in the federal debt.

The federal debt increased from $13 trillion on June 1, 2010 to an incredible $14 trillion on December 31, 2010. With the United States debt ceiling set at $14.294 trillion we are headed into troubled waters. The spending policies of the current administration must be stopped.

The sooner the administration figures out that the enemy is the bureaucracy and the wasteful spending, not the other party, the better off the country will be.

The first thing a bureaucracy does when attacked is to "circle the wagons" to protect itself.

The only way to stop this entrenched culture of waste is via the budget process. You need to take immediate steps to eliminate funding for non-value added programs.

The government could save billions of dollars by eliminating non-value-added federal civilian training and abolishing the Defense Acquisition Workforce Improvement Act of 1990.

We need to eliminate federal civilian training waste, bureaucracies that support these efforts, and realigning resources to support mission work. My perception is that useless civilian training not Soldier support has become the top priority of Army executives.

We also need to eliminate the use of government time and money for employees seeking educational degrees. Employees interested in self-improvement should do this on their own time and dime. Mission work not homework needs to be the priority. Review requirements for mandatory training and reduce this level of effort by 50%.

Other Recommendations:

- Eliminate the Installation Management Command which has increased the cost of operating military bases and the Army's special installations and return control back to Commanders who have a vested interest in their installations.

- Reduce the federal workforce by 30% - immediate hiring freeze and offer the "mother of all buyouts" - $100K and you will see many federal employees retire. Then for every three federal employees that retire hire one. Think about the savings the government will realize. Again only hire one back for every three that leave. You must then combine this with an intense effort to eliminate the "fluff" in federal employment (wasteful training, useless reviews, and redundant organizations). Implement an immediate reduction in the pay of all government employees by 25%. This will help many of the government employees decide that there might be a better way of earning income. Use the same formula and only hire one employee for every three that leave. There is way too much waste in the federal government.

- You must also re-vamp the federal classification system to avoid "high grade creep". I am convinced that the journeyman level for federal positions needs to be a GS-12 not a GS-13. GS-13s and above should be team leaders or first-line supervisors.

- Being politically correct, while the nation I love continues to sink into a fiscal abyss doesn't make any sense. The response to cutting federal waste needs to be aggressive and swift. It is time the Congress stepped up to the plate before the debt ceiling is reached. That will not be very many months as we are currently within $294 billion from reaching the ceiling.

THE UNITED STATES DEBT

The Congress now sworn in brings with it a new group of fiscally and socially conservative lawmakers -- a good portion of them elected as part of the Tea Party momentum currently reverberating through the Republican Party. Their campaign rhetoric of limited and financially responsible government clearly struck a chord with voters during the campaigns.

The Republicans were not even in control of the House of Representatives when the Associated Press started jumping into declaring that the Republican Congress is breaking promises? Two years into the job and the Associated Press fell far short of reporting any of the back door policies the Democrats were up to despite the fact they were clearly not in the best interest of all Americans. If it were not for the Tea party I doubt the Associated Press would have reported any of the anger most Americans had against the previous Democratic Congress. Seems obvious on which side the Associate Press is on and how they want the Republican Congress to fail. Yet we hear nothing on Nancy Pelosi's speech outlining lies about saving the USA many dollars just before Boehner took the gavel. Pelosi still wants to hang on despite the fact Members of Congress want her out.

By merely making the legislators attach a specific citation of the Constitution that gives them the power to pass said law will probably cut spending almost immediately. It will also make the new spending tougher to come by. I would also like them to take a complete hatchet to the current spending conducted by the Federal government and try to attach a Constitutional citation to each one. Then we could go after all of the duplicitous spending by making each program state in specific detail what their responsibilities are. If there are overlapping areas then we can combine and shred a department. We can also shed all of the departments that do nothing like the department of energy and all of the czars.

The Trade Deficit Contributing to the Debt

At this time in America's history we need a President that understands the 21st century economic policies and one that will uphold the Constitution and the laws of the United States of America. The American people can not settle for anything less. Contact your representatives and make sure that they vote for the policies that are critical to the country and ones that will vote on what the citizens want.

How serious is the trade deficit to the United States? What can we do to reduce or eliminate the amount of goods that are shipped into the United States?

The most important thing that the United States can do is reduce the amount of petroleum products that are imported into the country every year. Stop importing goods that can and should be "Made in USA" I find it hard to believe that the citizens of America can not make their own clothes instead on importing them from third world countries. The trade deficit would go down and the Americans could be put back to work.

The President advocates the support of building more wind energy systems. Does he realize that the propellers for all of these are being shipped in from China? Why not support building facilities in the United States that can make the propellers? It would reduce the trade deficit and have an added benefit of creating jobs in our own country.

There are too many individuals that are waiting for the federal government to resolve our economic problems. We all need to understand that the federal government can not continue to subsidize our countries over consumption of goods and services which will eventually bankrupt the government. Our economy will not return to normal until we reinstate manufacturing in America. By restructuring the manufacturing system in America it will automatically provide for growth in the economy.

In the last recessions the trade deficit has played a major role in the recessions. The current trade deficit reached $4.2 trillion. This was a very large amount of money that has disappeared from the United States economy. This was a major contributing factor in the economic failure of 2008. The continued increase on the trade deficit is going to cause a reduction in economic gains instead of improving them. We well see more unemployment and more Americans are going to loose their homes. This is going to happen time and time again until the manufacturing sector of our economy is reinstated.

The number one long term economic crisis for our economy is the trade deficit and the illegal immigrations. If they are left unchecked they will reduce America to a second rate power and a third world underclass society saddled with a very large federal deficit. Economically over the long term illegal immigration will destroy community safety nets unless something is done to correct the problem. It is already out of control.

The long term strategy of corporate America is to increase profit and jobs outside of America and reduce jobs in the United States. Economically, America's middle class is at severe risk of slipping backward. The downsizing in America started with outsourcing of our manufacturing jobs.

Outsourcing and the trade deficit are parts of an economic puzzle hidden behind import cost, shipping cost, insurance cost, wholesale and retail mark-up. The trade deficit is a direct subtraction from the GDP. The larger the trade deficit is each year the more it will drive the GDP into a negative growth.

The economic clock is ticking faster in the 21st century and we can not afford the luxury of having individuals in offices who do not understand 21st century economic. The illegals and the trade deficit will cause irreversible harm to our system if left unchecked. We need an overhaul of the federal, state and local governments. If history is of any value the New York Times in 1929 printed probably the number one reason for the stock market crash and eventually the depression was started when foreign investors pulled their investments out of the stock market. There are other similarities to the 1929 crash too. The Federal Reserve borrowed money for two years and poured it into the economy. The stock market crashed; there was a decline in GDP, the number of new jobs decreased, and the dollar declined worldwide.

According to the latest statistics from the United States International Trade Commission, United States imports of crude oil amounted to $60.4 billion for the first 4 months of 2010. That figure represents a 65.4% increase over the $36.5 billion that America spent on crude petroleum imports from January to April 2009. If that pace continues, total crude oil imports will cost an estimated $181 billion for 2010 which would be America's second highest expenditure on imported crude over the past 10 years. The total oil bill for 2010 will have been exceeded only by the $259.3 billion bill spent on imported crude oil during 2008.

These crude oil purchases would not be required if we developed the natural resources that are in our own country. How can we Americans be so stupid as to let one group of citizens have so much control over our country? The number of jobs that would be created would include: trucking, construction, engineering, housing, service, accommodations, refining, manufacturing, and many others to support the exploration industry. When the government starts to produce its own crude to eliminate the need for imported oil we will be able to install a reasonable tax increase per gallon of 10 cents and we will generate $17.922 billion in revenue. Take the 4,267,110,000 barrels of crude oil during 2009 times the 42 gallons per barrel and the tax it at 10 cents a gallon. When you figure that the average American uses 100 gallons per month the cost per individual is only $10.00. I would rather pay the extra few dollars and help get my country back to respectability and eliminate the deficits. That sure would be a lot better than sending $181 billion to the foreign countries around the world.

That would be in addition to the amount saved by not having to purchase crude oil from the Middle East and other countries. A great start to create a balanced budget. That would be a major improvement to our economic system and our balance of trade deficit.

The Congress needs to take control of our country and initiate legislation that will open up the exploration into all parts of the United States. The country just can not afford to waste our resources to save a few trees. We can build additional sections of our beautiful parks after the exploration has been completed. This will provide more usable recreation areas instead of just vast wildernesses.

Another aspect of the exploration is the amount of income tax that would be generated and the American companies would be paid the $372,646 billion instead of sending it to the foreign countries. If the production companies return a 15% net operating profit that they have to pay income tax on it will generate $19.565 billion. The production companies could pay to their employees 20% of the revenue to cover expenses which would generate $74.529 billion that would go directly into the economy. The social security and Medicare tax deductions along would generate an additional $11.179 billion in tax revenue for the government. We are not even taking into consideration the capital expenditures and the benefits to the local economies. This part of the equation will generate a total of $30.744 billion in revenue to the federal government.

Fuel taxes in the United States vary by state. For the first quarter of 2009, the mean state gasoline tax is 27.2 cents per US gallon, plus 18.4 cents per US gallon federal tax making the total 45.6 cents per US gallon. For diesel, the mean state tax is 26.6 cents per US gallon plus an additional 24.4 cents per US gallon federal tax making the total 50.8 cents US per gallon. There are also a few states that charge sales tax on top of the excise taxes and the retail price.

REMOVE THE GOVERNMENT FROM BUSINESS ACTIVITIES

The federal government needs to be removed from all types of activities that could be accomplished by the private sector of the economy. When the private sector is allowed to perform the services that the government performs the budget deficit will be reduced. Think about it? When the government performs the services they have to pay the employees and those funds come from the taxpayers. This creates an increase in the government expenses due to their continued insistence that they need to be part of unions. When the private sector performs these same functions they generate tax revenue for the government. This increases the government revenues and creates employment in the private sector that will help reduce unemployment. The private sector would be able to hire more people than the government since they will not be paying excessive union wages and benefits that the government employees are receiving. Additionally, the quality of the service is going to increase since these businesses will be trying to make profits and that will only happen when they perform. When their employees do not perform they can be terminates without any union interference. There are plenty of agencies of the federal government that could be abolished and turned over to the private sector of the economy. The government has grown too large and is trying to run every phase of the citizen's lives.

The Budget and Deficit

The government must be required to balance the budget and eliminate the deficit spending policies that have created approximately $14 trillion in federal deficit through December 31, 2010.

The most important thing that the new Congress can do would be to prepare legislation that makes it a law to have a balanced budget. The 2011 proposed budget that the President has developed has a deficit of $1.267 trillion dollars which is 8.3% of the GDP. What is amazing is that in the proposed federal budget there is discretionary spending that is $1.3 trillion which is 33.9% of the entire amount of $3.834 trillion expenditures for the year. Why are we giving these departments what is considered a blank check instead of itemizing what they are going to spend our money on?

We are concerned with the direction that the economy, unemployment, spending, immigration and lack of transparency with the current administration. It is time that the voting citizens voice their opinions and vote for representation that will vote for programs that are for "We the People, By the People and For the People".

The excessive federal spending programs have to stop. We need a balanced budget in the United States. We need to enact programs that will reduce the unemployment and stop the illegals from entering the United States. The United States needs to be firm on completing the border fence and enforcing the laws with regard to illegals. There can not be amnesty for the 20,000,000 illegals that are already in the United States.

We are hoping that America can reduce the size of the government and can get back to government for the people.

The federal government could cut into the deficit without sacrificing our security, services or dignity by reducing the discretionary spending in the 2011 proposed budget by only ten percent. (10%) The government could reduce the deficit by $130.068 billion by passing this one austerity program for the year ending on September 30, 2011.

All of us citizens have had to reduce our budget by a whole lot more that the 10 percent. The government needs to stop the spending.

In a time when 47% of American households did not pay any federal income tax in 2009 (according to the IRS) and with real unemployment running close to 20%, and when our national debt just shot up 36% in 18 month... the big news is tax cuts? Hell the federal employees already gave themselves a tax cut - 638 federal workers on Capitol Hill owed the IRS $9.3 Million in back taxes. How about the Department of Homeland Security? – Within that department there were 4,856 people who owed the IRS a combined total of $37,012,174. Another 41 people inside the White House owed the IRS $831,055 in back taxes. In Tim Geithner's Treasury Department, 1,204 employees owed $7,670,814. Over at the Justice Department, which is so busy enforcing other laws and suing Arizona, 1,971 employees still owed $14,350,152 in overdue taxes.

People need to wake up and stop this attack on the "rich". At least they are paying their taxes.

The following is printed from the Constitution of the United States of America.

The Constitution of the United States

Section 7 - Revenue Bills, Legislative Process, Presidential Veto

All bills for raising Revenue shall originate in the House of Representatives; but the Senate may propose or concur with Amendments as on other Bills.

Every Bill which shall have passed the House of Representatives and the Senate, shall, before it become a Law, be presented to the President of the United States; If he approve he shall sign it, but if not he shall return it, with his Objections to that House in which it shall have originated, who shall enter the Objections at large on their Journal, and proceed to reconsider it. If after such Reconsideration two thirds of that House shall agree to pass the Bill, it shall be sent, together with the Objections, to the other House, by which it shall likewise be reconsidered, and if approved by two thirds of that House, it shall become a Law. But in all such Cases the Votes of both Houses shall be determined by Yeas and Nays, and the Names of the Persons voting for and against the Bill shall be entered on the Journal of each House respectively. If any Bill shall not be returned by the President within ten Days (Sundays excepted) after it shall have been presented to him, the same shall be a Law, in like Manner as if he had signed it, unless the Congress by their Adjournment prevent its Return, in which Case it shall not be a Law.

Every Order, Resolution, or Vote to which the Concurrence of the Senate and House of Representatives may be necessary (except on a question of Adjournment) shall be presented to the President of the United States; and before the Same shall take Effect, shall be approved by him, or being disapproved by him, shall be re-passed by two thirds of the Senate and House of Representatives, according to the Rules and Limitations prescribed in the Case of a Bill.

PROGRAM FOUR:

QUALIFICATIONS FOR CONGRESS

THE UNITED STATES NEED TO ESTABLISH QUALIFICATIONS FOR HOLDING THE OFFICES OF THE PRESIDENT, ALL MEMBERS OF THE CONGRESS AND THE ATTORNEY GENERAL OF THE UNITED STATES OF AMERICA.

The reading of the Constitution of the United States was done for the first time in 222 years. What has taken them so long? We know by the types of legislation that has been passed that most of the Congress did not know what was in the Constitution.

They should have administered an exam afterward, to see if anyone understood what was read and then the results should have been entered into the congressional record along with official reprimands for any poor or failing grades.

I find this hysterical that Nancy Pelosi actually read from the Constitution. She is the same one who, when asked where in the Constitution the federal government was given the authority to force people to buy health insurance, just looked at the man as if he were crazy and said "Are you serious?" Yeah, Nancy, he was serious and so are the Republicans.

Qualifications of Congressmen

The members that serve in the House of Representatives and the Senators should all be held to qualification standards to hold their positions. These standards should be for newcomers and the holdovers from prior elections. All the members should have a sixty day grace period to become qualified.

Requirements for all Members of Congress

What about a testing requirement?

The members of Congress and the House of Representatives would have to pass sum sort of licensing procedure to make sure that they know a little bit about what they are doing. We have to pass tests to do something as simple as driving an automobile, sell insurance, sell securities, sell real estate and many other professions. Why not make our representatives know something about the United States Constitution and the Amendments? A test could be made up of a battery of 500 questions and everyone would have to take an examination containing 100 questions and have a passing score of at least 80%. These questions could be made up by a group of law professors at our leading institutions of higher learning and be put into a question bank and the 100 would be randomly chosen by computer to make sure that the people taking the test would not know which questions that they would be getting. They would actually have to know the United States Constitution and the Amendments in order to pass the test. All current members of both houses will be required to pass the same test within a 60 day period

What about requiring payment of all taxes?

All members of Congress, the House of Representatives, the President, the Vice President, the heads of the Justice Departments and every other department head that is appointed by the President will be required to show proof that they do not owe any State Income Taxes, Federal Income Taxes or local property taxes. This also includes any member of the staffs. No exceptions.

The following formation will confirm the need for enforcing the payment of all income taxes prior to appointment to an office in the federal government:

TAXES OWED BY CONGRESSIONAL EMPLOYEES ARE $9,300,000...

A news article on September 9, 2010 by Politics Daily reported that there were 638 congressional employees that owed $9.3 million in back taxes.

The paper used Internal Revenue Service data to determine that about 4% of the workforce on Capital Hill owed overdue federal income taxes. That $9.3 million was a small fraction of the over a $1 billion owed by federal employees across government.

It is unknown if any Senators or United States Representatives are among these taxpayers. The Post indicated the average unpaid tax bill in the Senate was $12,787, while the House average was $15,498.

IT GETS BETTER!! The Post found that 41 employees of the Executive Office of the President of the United States owed a total of $831,000 in overdue back federal taxes.

Representative Jason Chaffetza (R-Utah) said. "If you're on the federal payroll and you're not paying your taxes, you should be fired."

Let's Hope that they get legislation passed that will enforce the payment of all taxes or the employee is fired. That includes all the members of the Congress and the President and their appointees.

It appears that the majority of the American citizens are going to be looking for representatives that want to represent the citizens of the United States.

That is why it is so important that the representatives are screened to make sure that they have the qualities that are required to be one of the 535 individuals that are making the decisions for the remaining 308,700,000 Americans.

What about absolute proof of citizenship?

All members of Congress, the House of Representatives, the President, the Vice President, the heads of the Justice Departments and every other department head that is appointed by the President will be required to show absolute proof that they are American Citizens. This will be in the form of a certified copy of the birth certificate from the hospital where they were born. In addition, all the above mentioned officers will provide proof of their educational and military background. No exceptions.

These requirements should be investigated prior to allowing anyone to run for a public office. We need to know that the people that are running for offices in our government are qualified and proper to hold the office that they are running for. That should be both at the State and Federal level.

Every person that is running for public office must be required to provide accurate and complete financial disclosure statements.

What about law abiding representation?

There should be term limits placed on both the Congress and the House of Representatives. A balanced budget should be required every year. If the budget is not balanced then lower the wages of every Senator and Congressman by 20 percent. Most of them are very rich and it will not change their lifestyle. When a bill is passed that will effect the American citizen then it should apply to the members of Congress and the House of Representatives. The honor of being a Senator or Congressman should not be a lifetime career.

Eliminate all pork projects that are added to legislation for the benefit of a few instead of the entire country. If the add on to a bill is not qualified to pass on its own merit then it probable is not for the good of all the people of the United States.

The campaign rules need to be fixed. All politicians should be required to use the same amount of funds in their election campaign. The government provides matching funds which will even the playing field. The current system just promotes the buying of votes from the candidate that is able to secure the most funds. The exceptions could be anyone using their personal wealth to pay for their campaign. If a candidate is committed enough to spend their money to have the chance to further the development and betterment of the United States should be applauded. They are not living off the rest of the citizens. Think about it, would you spend your own money? That takes real dedication and they are not looking for a handout.

The government needs to start enforcing the laws against kickbacks of any time. That goes for the President, all the Senators, Representatives and all other appointed officials in the government. It also applies to the lobbyist and group caught trying to buy votes on any legislation.

There should be a cooling off period after any legislation is written so that every member that is required to vote has had an opportunity to read the entire bill. This will give every Senator or Representative an opportunity to ask questions about the bill before the vote is taken. We can not allow for any more of the legislation being passed like the healthcare bill that Nancy Pelosi recommended passing so that the members could find out what was in the bill. That will go down as one of the stupidest remarks ever uttered by the Chairman of the House of Representatives.

The government needs to quit forcing legislation upon the citizens that are against the will of the American citizens. No more back office deals.

You are not going to believe the following. It is proof that what we are suggesting about the members of the Congress knowing about the

Constitution of the United States. This article was published on January 14, 2011 and clearly demonstrates our position on qualifications.

Opinion: Elected Officials Flunk Constitution Quiz

Jan 14, 2011 – 6:00 AM

Special to AOL News

When the Republican House leadership decided to start the 112th Congress with a reading of the United States Constitution, the decision raised complaints in some quarters that it was little more than a political stunt. The New York Times even called it a "presumptuous and self-righteous act."

That might be true, if you could be sure that elected officials actually know something about the Constitution. But it turns out that many don't.

In fact, elected officials tend to know even *less* about key provisions of the Constitution than the general public.

For five years now, the Intercollegiate Studies Institute has been conducting a national survey to gauge the quality of civic education in the country. We've surveyed more than 30,000 Americans, most of them college students, but also a random sample of adults from all educational and demographic backgrounds.

Included in the adult sample was a small subset of Americans (165 in all) who, when asked, identified themselves as having been "successfully elected to government office at least once in their life" -- which can include federal, state or local offices.

The survey asks 33 basic civics questions, many taken from other nationally recognized instruments like the United States Citizenship Exam. It also asks 10 questions related to the United States Constitution.

So what did we find? Well, to put it simply, the results are not pretty.

Elected officials at many levels of government, not just the federal government, swear an oath to "uphold and protect" the United States Constitution.

But those elected officials who took the test scored an average 5 percentage points lower than the national average (49 percent vs. 54 percent), with ordinary citizens outscoring these elected officials on each constitutional question.

Examples:

- Only 49 percent of elected officials could name all three branches of government, compared with 50 percent of the general public.

- Only 46 percent knew that Congress, not the president, has the power to declare war -- 54 percent of the general public knows that.

- Just 15 percent answered correctly that the phrase "wall of separation" appears in Thomas Jefferson's letters -- not in the United States Constitution -- compared with 19 percent of the general public.

- And only 57 percent of those who've held elective office know what the Electoral College does, while 66 percent of the public got that answer right. (Of elected officials, 20 percent thought the Electoral College was a school for "training those aspiring for higher political office.")

Overall, our sample of elected officials averaged a failing 44 percent on the entire 33-question test, 5 percentage points lower than the national average of 49 percent.

The fact that our elected representatives know even less about America's history and institutions than the typical citizen (who doesn't know much either) is troubling indeed, but perhaps helps explain the lack of constitutional discipline often displayed by our political class at every level of our system.

Given this dismal performance, it would seem that last week's House reading of the Constitution shouldn't be described "presumptuous and self-righteous," but as a necessary national tutorial for all elected officials.

In fact, we can only hope that this trend of Constitution reading will continue to sweep the nation and states. After all, there are 50 state constitutions as well.

When elected officials take an oath "to protect and defend the Constitution," shouldn't they know what they are swearing to?

*Richard Brake is co-chairman of the Intercollegiate Studies Institute's National Civic Literacy Board. For more details regarding the ISI's past and current civic literacy studies and to **take the test** online, go to **www.americancivicliteracy.org**.*

Are you smarter than an elected official?

If you can correctly answer five or more of these basic Constitution-related questions, congratulations! You're smarter than the average elected official! (Answers are below -- but no peeking!)

1) What are the three branches of government?

A. executive, legislative, judicial

B. executive, legislative, military

C. bureaucratic, military, industry

D. federal, state, local

2) What part of the government has the power to declare war?

A. Congress

B. the president

C. the Supreme Court

D. the Joint Chiefs of Staff

3) In the area of United States foreign policy, Congress shares power with the:

A. president

B. Supreme Court

C. state governments

D. United Nations

4) The United States Electoral College:

A. trains those aspiring for higher political office

B. was established to supervise the first televised presidential debates

C. is otherwise known as the U.S. Congress

D. is a constitutionally mandated assembly that elects the president

E. was ruled undemocratic by the Supreme Court

5) What impact did the Anti-Federalists have on the United States Constitution?

A. their arguments helped lead to the adoption of the Bill of Rights

B. their arguments helped lead to the abolition of the slave trade

C. their influence ensured that the federal government would maintain a standing army

D. their influence ensured that the federal government would have the power to tax

6) The phrase that in America there should be a "wall of separation" between church and state appears in:

A. George Washington's Farewell Address

B. the Mayflower Compact

C. the Constitution

D. the Declaration of Independence

E. Thomas Jefferson's letters

7) The Bill of Rights explicitly prohibits:

A. prayer in public school

B. discrimination based on race, sex, or religion

C. the ownership of guns by private individuals

D. establishing an official religion for the United States

E. the president from vetoing a line item in a spending bill

8) Identify one right or freedom below guaranteed by the first amendment.

A. Right to bear arms

B. Due process

C. Religion

D. Right to counsel

9) Under our Constitution, some powers belong to the federal government. What is one power of the federal government listed below?

A. Make treaties

B. Make zoning laws

C. Maintain prisons

D. Establish standards for doctors and lawyers

10) Who is the commander in chief of the U.S. military?

A. Secretary of the army

B. Secretary of state

C. President

D. Chairman of the Joint Chiefs

Answer key:

1) A; 2) A; 3) A; 4) D; 5) A; 6) E; 7) D; 8) C; 9) A; 10) C

PROGRAM FIVE:

OUR VAST NATURAL RESOURCES:

The American Citizens Political Action Committee will be promoting the passage of legislation that will authorize the exploration of our natural resources in the Alaskan Natural Wildlife Refuge and the Rocky Mountain Regions of the United States. There is no reason for the United States to continue increasing our deficit every year by purchasing crude oil and natural gas from foreign countries when we can produce the product in the United States.

When we produce the oil and natural gas from the resources of the United States we will provide for the countries vast consumption but we will decrease our national deficit each year. How simple can it be? We need people with common sense in Washington and not people with Doctors Degrees. History has shown that some of the most highly educated individuals do not have one iota of common sense and are not able to listen to what the American public want. The truth about producing our natural resources is following.

Not everyone is against the production of our natural resources. Some are just clinging to the past. Oil has been produced for about 80 years. Other sources of energy are in fact expensive when you compare it to oil. And that's why no one really wants to do it right now. But eventually we will have to do it because we will run out of oil. I honestly think solar is the way to go. However, it's a very limited resource. It's only good for a few things whereas oil can be used for over 6000 different products throughout the world.

Oil is the energy source in our lifetime. Stop and think about that for a moment. It is the source of energy in our lifetime. We need oil, we must have it. It is the source of so many products. Did you know plastic requires oil? Oil is here to stay. At least in our lifetime it is. I understand that in the future other energy sources will take over but for now oil is king.

The Gulf oil spill is a good example of the misinformed leading the misinformed. I hope everyone who thinks this way can afford to pay $10.00 per gallon for gas. You have been lied to by the militant environmentalist movement. The spill, while regrettable, certainly could have been minimized if our leaders would have taken the proper steps to solve the situation early. The truth is they wanted it to be this bad so that they could further their agenda to bring America to its knees through the green movement.

The Obama administration gave British Petroleum 274 passes on failed safety inspections in the last year alone. So who is really at fault? You won't hear about these facts being reported by the main stream media. The main stream media is blinding you and they haven't had to work very hard to accomplish the fact. They lie straight to your face yet you are too lazy to go get the facts yourself.

Information gathered from the biological, seismic and geological studies was used to complete a Legislative Environmental Impact Statement (LEIS) that described the potential impacts of oil and gas development. This LEIS study included the Secretary's final report and recommendation, and was submitted to Congress in 1987. The report concluded that oil development and production in the 1002 Area would have major effects on the Porcupine Caribou herd and muskoxen. Major effects were defined as "widespread, long-term change in habitat availability or quality which would likely modify natural abundance or distribution of species." Moderate effects were expected for wolves, wolverine, polar bears, snow geese, seabirds and shorebirds, arctic grayling and coastal fish. Major restrictions on subsistence activities by Kaktovik residents would also be expected. In the report, the Secretary of Interior recommended that Congress authorize an oil and gas leasing program that would avoid unnecessary adverse effects on the environment.

Congress failed to act on the recommendation, first in 1989 following the Exxon Valdez oil spill, and again in 1991 when a provision to open the Arctic Refuge to development was dropped from the National Energy Policy Act. In 1995, Congress passed budget legislation that included a provision to allow drilling in the Refuge. Citing a desire to protect biological and wilderness values, President Clinton vetoed the bill.

The estimated oil reserves in the Artic Refuge's 1002 Area are in excess of 30 billion barrels that could be recoverable. With oil prices over $80.00 per barrel and going higher it would be in the best interest of the United States to commence drilling in this area. These reserves would reduce the national debt and provide the United States with independence from foreign oil producers. Every barrel of oil that the United States can produce eliminates one that has to be imported.

Newer technologies that are applied today in Alaska's expanding North

Slope oil fields include directional drilling that allows for multiple well heads on smaller drill pads; the re-injection of drilling wastes into the ground, which replaces surface reserve pits; better delineation of oil reserves using 3-dimensional seismic surveys, which has reduced the number of dry holes; and use of temporary ice pads and ice roads for conducting exploratory drilling and construction in the winter. As the oil fields expand east and west, additional oil reserves are consequently being tapped from smaller satellite fields that rely on the existing infrastructure at Prudhoe Bay and Kuparuk.

Oil shipments to the United States from Venezuela declined from 49 million barrels in February 1999, when Chavez took office, to 31.9 million barrels during the same month last year. Think how difficult it would be for Venezuela to carry out any of Chavez's plans when the United States finally has a president that will cut off the purchases from Venezuela altogether. The United States could reduce the amount of money spent for foreign oil by $25.5 billion dollars per month. That will make a very nice dent in our balance of payments with foreign countries. That amounts to $306 billion per year which is about one third of the projected deficit per year. Just think about this. When we become free from foreign oil altogether we will have just about balanced the federal budget.

The President does not support developing the natural resources of the United States the budget also eliminates funding for fossil fuel development. The President needs to understand that all the wind farm development he is pushing uses products such as the propellers that are not produced in the United States. How does that create production jobs for the Americans?

Nowhere in the President's proposed budget was there any mention of reducing the independence on foreign oil. There is also nothing mentioned about developing our own natural resources. The President's proposals are more on the lines of spend, spend and then spend some more to develop green energy sources that should be funded by corporate enterprises. The oil industry will fund the development of our natural resources in the state of Alaska and the Rocky Mountain Region of the United States. That would be proper management of our resources and reduce the national deficit at the same time. Let private businesses fund their own green energy ideas and not the taxpayers.

Here are the Obama administrations answers to our energy problems. These are directly from the President's proposed budget for the year ending September 30, 2011.

Because we know the nation that leads in clean energy will be the nation that leads the world, the Budget creates the incentives to build a new clean energy economy—from new loan guarantees that will encourage a range of renewable energy efforts and new nuclear power plants to spurring the development of clean energy on Federal lands. More broadly, the Budget makes critical investments that will ensure that we continue to lead the world in new fields and industries: doubling research and development funding in key physical sciences agencies; expanding broadband networks across our country; and working to promote American exports abroad.

Could there be more to the cap and trade then is disclosed. Just who is going to benefit the most from the cap and trade? The history of that bill needs to be investigated before the Congress passes the bill.

PROGRAM SIX:

EARMARK LEGISLATION

American Citizens Political Action Committee will press the representatives of both parties in Congress to pass legislation that will abolish all earmark legislation.

Although Senate Republicans have vowed to halt the practice, Senate Majority Leader Harry Reid defended it as the obligation of every member of Congress.

"I believe, personally, we have a constitutional obligation, a responsibility, to do congressionally direct the spending. I do not feel comfortable turning that over to the people downtown," Reid said, referring to federal agencies that would assume the responsibility of designating federal funds in the absence of congressional direction. "So I am not going to back off of bringing stuff back to Nevada."

The Congress needs to pass legislation that bans all earmark attachments to any piece of legislation that is proposed in both houses. Every bill that is presented should be able to stand on the merits of the legislation. If it can't be passed without bribing the members with pork the bill probably was not for the benefit of the people of the United States.

On November 30, 2010, The United States Senate voted 56 to 39 to continue to allow congressional earmarking, the practice that lets individual lawmakers designate federal funds for specific projects, usually in their home states. The Senators just can not get it straight about what the voting citizens of the United States want. The citizens want truth in legislation and that will only come when each and every piece of legislation is passed on the merits of the bill. The earmarks just lead to corruption in the Congress.

Although Senate Republicans recently adopted a nonbinding resolution to prevent Republican senators from requesting or supporting earmarks, the bill proposed Tuesday -- by two Democrats and two Republicans -- would have formally changed Senate rules to make it impossible for the chamber to move any bill with an earmark attached.

Despite the GOP caucus' official stand against the practice earlier this month, eight Republicans joined a majority of Democrats to keep earmarking alive, including Alaska Sen. Lisa Murkowski, who defended the practice on the campaign trail this year, arguing that the millions of earmarked dollars that her state gets help with everything from air mail delivery for remote islands to basic infrastructure projects. Also voting yes were Republicans Susan Collins (Maine), Jim Inhofe (Okla.), Richard Shelby (Ala.), Richard Lugar (Ind.), Robert Bennett (Utah), George Voinovich (Ohio), and Thad Cochran (Miss.), the top Republican on the Senate Appropriations Committee.

Democrats were no more united than the GOP on the issue. Although Senate Majority Leader Harry Reid defended congressional earmarks earlier this month as the constitutional obligation of every member of Congress, six Democrats bucked Reid and voted to put an end to practice, at least temporarily.

Russ Feingold (Wis.), Evan Bayh (Ind.), Michael Bennet (Colo.), and Mark Warner (Va.) joined Claire McCaskill (Mo.) and Mark Udall (Colo.) in voting against earmarks. McCaskill and Udall introduced the measure with GOP Senators Tom Coburn (Okla.) and John McCain (Ariz.), two longtime critics of pork-barrel spending.

The issue has roiled both Democrats and Republicans this year as they balanced the chance to send federal funds back to their states and districts with the increasing anger of American voters, who have complained more and more that federal spending is out of control.

Banning earmarks would decrease the budget deficit due to the fact that a large portion of the earmarks would not pass as stand alone bills that only benefit an individual state. The Republicans in the House of Representatives need to bring this to a vote again after the Democrats are removed from their office.

The vast majority of the American taxpayers voted to eliminate all earmarks. The Republicans had better get off the stump and propose legislation that bans all earmarks in January 2011. Then if the President veto's the bill it will be another strike against his re-election goals for 2012.

Senator Richard Durbin (Ill.), the second-ranking Democrat in the Senate and a member of the Appropriations Committee, argued before Tuesday's vote that senators are already making voluntary efforts to increase transparency in earmarking and that the effort is "virtually unprecedented."

The Citizens against Government Waste puts out an annual "Congressional Pig Book" that listed 9,129 projects at a cost of $16.5 billion in 2010.

I would like to see a total breakdown of the $800 billion stimulus bill to include each and every project that was in the bill. How many pork projects were attached to the bill to get it passed. The government needs to provide a complete accounting for each project that was funded by the bill. That includes engineering cost, labor cost, material cost and all other expenses. When the accounting is received it could reveal just how many jobs were created for non union members that were not employed by the contractors who received the project money. How many jobs did this massive spending bill create for the unemployed?

The Obama administration needs to make a full disclosure about the healthcare legislation. The citizens of the United States have the God given right to know what pork projects were attached to this bill. We already know that the requirement to have businesses prepare Form 1099's on every business that they sell or buy over $600 from. What other garbage attachments are on the healthcare bill? All of the pork attachments need to be repealed immediately.

Harry Reid the leader of the Senate started his campaigning in Nevada by bragging about his ability to bring hundreds of millions of dollars in federal pork back to the state of Nevada.

The Congress has created a federal government that's too big and too expensive. Every political candidate should swear off the earmarks. Congress needs to know that many of the systems or manifestations of the pork spending, which is the political lubricant that keeps this big machine going and keeps it growing. We need to decrease the size of government and not provide methods of making the government larger. Eliminate all pork spending.

Could it be that the pork problem is going to be heard? The anti-earmark candidates promise to shake up a Capitol culture in which earmarking is seen by most lawmakers as a birthright. In the House, Minority Leader John Boehner, R-Ohio, who has never sought an earmark, earlier this year orchestrated a Republican rules change in which the party swore off earmarks. Now they need to pass legislation that makes it illegal to have earmarks.

PROGRAM SEVEN:

EARLY CAMPAIGNING:

President Obama is already campaigning for his re-election on 2012. This type of rhetoric will not be accepted by the average thinking citizen of the United States. Clearly what the President needs to do is try and come up with some real programs that will reduce the real unemployment rate in the United States. This constant spinning of the facts has become absolutely insulting and boring to the citizens. The President is hoping that he will be able to spin enough garbage to the uneducated minorities in the country and they will forget about what has actually happened during the past two years and the next two years. If you can not run on your record then you have to try and create false hope for the lemmings.

Unfortunately for the average American citizen that does not rely on entitlement programs we are facing a difficult task of overcoming the Hispanic, Black and other minority groups that are living of the entitlement programs. In the 2008 elections over 90% of the black voters in the country voted for Obama because he was black. The Hispanic population voted for Obama by a 70% majority due to his promises on immigration.

This country needs to return to voting for the candidate that will present programs that will benefit every American. Not just promises, but real plans on how the programs are going to be implemented. Quit the rhetoric and get to the real facts. Let the American citizens know what you are really made of and how your programs are going to work for the people. God Bless America.

Obama: Positive 'Trend Is Clear' for Economy on the Upswing and Moving in the Right Direction:

President Obama said that the drop in joblessness and a batch of tax benefits extending into the New Year show that "the trend is clear" for an economy on the upswing. He urged Congress not to "re-fight the battles of the past two years" that took time away from the struggle to get the economy back on track.

The president used his weekly address to talk up the tax relief enacted by Congress in a bipartisan compromise last month and to put a positive light on the December jobs numbers, which showed unemployment dropping from 9.8 percent to 9.4 percent. But the report also revealed disappointing growth in hiring by private sector employers last month --103,000 positions, not enough to keep up with new applicants in the job market.

President Barack Obama sees a clear and encouraging trend on the economy, citing fresh reports showing private-sector job growth and lower unemployment.

"Now we know that these numbers can bounce around from month to month," Obama said. "But the trend is clear. We saw 12 straight months of private sector job growth -- the first time that's been true since 2006. The economy added 1.3 million jobs last year."

President Barack Obama sees a clear and encouraging trend on the economy, citing fresh reports showing private-sector job growth and lower unemployment.

He urged businesses to take advantage of provisions including one that allows businesses to write off 100 percent of their capital investment expenses in 2011. And the president said that the deal stands as an example of how Washington should work as he confronts a Congress where Republicans just assumed the majority in the House and expanded their ranks in the Senate.

The President failed to mention that the economy needs to create 350,000 jobs per month or 4.2 million jobs per year to keep up with the expanding growth in the number of workers entering the job market. The number the President was quoting will only lead to bigger problems in the unemployment market in the coming months.

Obama reminded Americans that thanks to the agreement on extending Bush-era tax cuts into 2011, payroll taxes will go down, many families will benefit from a $1.000 child tax credit, and businesses will be able to write off most of their capital investments for one year.

"Our fundamental mission must be to accelerate hiring and growth..." he said "I'm absolutely confident we will get there." He warned that "we can't re-fight battles of the past two years that distract us from the hard work of moving our economy forward. What we can't do is engage in the kinds of symbolic battles that so often consume Washington while the rest of America waits for us to solve problems."

The American Citizens Political Action Committee has recorded some comments concerning the Presidents latest radio broadcast. Now let's read what the citizens think about the President and his statements concerning the recovery in America. After we review the comments we will consolidate and format a plan on how to solve the systems.

Really, Mr. President, it's time to wake up from your dream world and come back to reality. You should figure out by now that saying it does not make it so.

Obama says economy moving in right direction he also said he would provide transparency in the government, he also said he would be a President of unification (unfortunately that's true for the Mexicans), he also said he would make cuts in government spending, he also said he wouldn't raise taxes....which lie should we discuss first?

103,000 jobs were added last month. 260,000 eligible workers stopped looking for work (Wall St. Journal, p. A12, 1/9/2011). Thus, like magic, we get an "improvement" in the unemployment rate. How does the President think we are making progress when the country needs to create 350,000 new jobs per month to keep up with the number of new citizens that are entering the workplace?

If I had an employee that never listened to my requests, never was reliable in their management of my the resources that I provided him, expected to continue to be employed until their dying day, and only cared about their own personal welfare I would fire them. Why do we not fire our Politicians for doing a horrific job with our resources and future? Why do we let them continue to seal our countries fate to fall to a 3rd world countries status? Without Dramatic change we are no more than 5 years away from our economies end.

Our country has lost its manufacturing core to other countries as well as the jobs to go with it and we have become the biggest debtor nation on earth. Now our retarded leaders seem bent on giving the United States to Mexico. What's up with that? Now they want to raise our debt limit to over 14 trillion dollars all the while our counties social programs are 75 trillion in the red. I could go on but I just wanted to point out that it is interesting how Obama is painting such a rosy picture.

"The private sector raised 103,000 more jobs in December". Yes and that was right after Obama compromised and signed the tax cut continuation to include the wealthy businesses for another two years like the Republicans had insisted on. Without those tax cuts for the big businesses, the businesses could not expand and make new job positions. I personally heard and read the big businesses announce expansion and new jobs right after Obama signed the compromise. So, thank you Republicans for foreseeing what was needed. I still say that big businesses tax cuts should be based on higher tax cuts for those who manufacture products in America and a lower tax cut for those who manufacture in other countries. We need manufacturing plants here in America providing more jobs, rather than sending the work to other countries.

Progress well that's quite a word I think to most Americans the word Progress means a great deal different then the way Obama means it. It might be his up bringing in different parts of the world it could be confused with the word progressive two simple words the only trouble is one is a move forward and the other is a move to bondage. If America allows the Democrats to use their meaning of the word then we as Americans will be going back to the future the future where Russia and Cuba lived in bliss but their people lost all resemblance of the need for freedom and free will and that is the progressive destruction of the American Spirit.

He spent the first two years of his presidency doing whatever he could to ruin our free market economy and turn us into a nanny state, and now he says we are moving in the right direction. I guess it all depends upon your perspective. Mine says we are continuing to go down hill with regulations galore and changes that do not benefit the average American. I want to get off this train.

Obama used to look so arrogant now he just looks like a broken man with no idea what to do his policies have done nothing but harm America if someone wanted to destroy our country our way of life they would have to copy what Obama has done for the last 19 months destroy from within that was the tactic that was written about in the 60's when the weather men and other anti-American groups were hoping to do what's funny well not funny is the same people who made up those groups of the 60's are not only around but insiders of Hussein Obama's inner circle Wake up America the enemy is here and laughing at all Americans. During The election for President Obama said he wants to fundamentally change America there is only one way to do that and it is to destroy our constitution. There are so many sheep following I have seen it spoke it before the election when he said he wanted to change America blinded by his charm arrogant smug its like he is so far above The average American One year ago he agreed even though the voted against it for both Iraq and Afghanistan but it took him over 6 months to actually start to send troops

You put this together with Pakistan refuses to fight the terrorists in the tribal region put this along with the United States giving them $7 billion on Friday October 22, 2010. Why is America allowing Obama to do this? Figure it out.

A deceptively dismal jobs report, combined with Federal Chairman Ben Bernanke's acknowledgement that it might be another five years before hiring fully recovers, put the final nail in the coffin Friday on

the Obama administration's claim that nearly $1 trillion in stimulus spending has rescued the economy.

Although the headline number is impressive, with unemployment falling from 9.8 percent to 9.4 percent, the number of new jobs created was a big disappointment and far lower than private forecasters had predicted only days ago.

President Barack Obama sees a clear and encouraging trend on the economy, citing fresh reports showing private-sector job growth and lower unemployment.

This proves the President is a "malignant narcissist and possibly a borderline psychotic" who actually believes that the American people will buy into his bizarre, offensive delusional lies.

Obama is like a slick used car salesman and he wants to sell you a busted used car with a "FULL FACTORY" warranty for repairs. And you know what? 50% of the American people are buying it, plus an extended warranty. The rest of us knew better two years ago not to trust this flim-flam of a man and his smooth talking ways.

Too bad all the created jobs went to Obama's precious "illegal immigrants". Wake up sheep, socialism doesn't work and it never did. They want to educate the illegals so they can not only take labor jobs but white collar jobs as well. If you haven't been affected by this ruse yet trust me, keep pushing for illegal immigrant rights and you will be. They have all but taken over blue collar industry and now they want to educate them so they can take over white collar industry and you dopes are leading the charge. You all say that he needs more time that 2 years isn't enough for what he took over from the last administration. However, Reagan took over a failed economy from Carter and in 2 years it wasn't fixed but the signs of recovery were extremely evident and things were undoubtedly going in the right direction which is not the case with Obama, things are decidedly worse and obviously heading in the wrong direction. He is clueless and that's the difference. Wake up sheep.

Wake up Obama you have been flying all over on your vacation while many Americans have suffer with unemployment and no hopes for any new jobs in the future because Washington has passed the NAFTA agreement without reading any thing in it this bill has put over 80 million Americans out of work. You jester in Washington doesn't have a clue. Hell the Congress doesn't even read the bills that they pass.

December jobs rise is normal for holiday season with temporary minimum wage jobs. This incompetent and his unfit crew love to crow and give themselves undue credit. Three dollars gas is not a move in the right direction and the economy is stagnant and will not improve anytime soon so do your best to hang on to what you got people till we can get this bumbling idiot out of office and someone who is able the job voted in.

The economy is moving in right direction. Since WWII, election of a Republican Congress has never been followed by high unemployment. In contrast, when Democrats controlled the House, unemployment was 6% or higher about half the time! This last election set us in the right direction.

Consumers and employers have been expecting the economy to get better ever since it became clear that Republicans were going to have a big win in the 2010 elections. Now, it's just a matter of time until the economy rebounds.

People can not pay rent or mortgage because the businesses shut down because the price of gas went so high and we are getting taken because the foreign oil is making them enough money to buy our properties. Think and wake up America.

It is amazing how the people who have never worked a day in their life have the BALLS to say they know what AVERAGE people are going through and what the AVERAGE person needs.

Is this guy on drugs!! 500,000 dropped from the unemployment rolls due to economic policies he pushed and we are going in the right direction? Only 103K new hires and that is only 2K per state think about it. This clown is a joke and a bad one at that. Why does he keep bashing Wall Street when Obama has many friends on Wall Street he

helped bail out? God what a liar, but of course the progressives will tell we are going in the right direction. What direction are they going and to what?

Obama is just expressing his own confidence in the Republican Party, now that they have taken over the House of Representatives not unlike most Americans. He knows that a big change is coming (including his own job). If hiring is in fact up, it is due to the results of the last election and the excitement of the American people over the prospect of un-doing the MESS that has been created by the current Administration.

You betcha Barry! And do you want to know why? Because America knows that you have effectively been put in a box, and will no longer be a threat to our economic well being in the near future. 2012 is just around the corner. I can't wait to be a member of a Christian Nation once again. The economy is in a shambles except for Wall Street as another Goldman Sacks man comes to run the White House. Banks are not lending, real estate is crashing and real unemployment is double digit. Meanwhile DC is printing money plundering the future of our children.

For all you out there who used to blame the high gasoline prices on Bush because he was "an oil man" what do you say about the rising cost NOW? Bush is no longer in the White House and your man Obama does not seem to be doing much to help us out. All he seems to care about is legalizing twenty-five million illegals, to pad the democrat vote.

We are moving right where he wants us to be dependant on government, entitlements, union payoffs, hostile government takeovers, poor economy, failing schools and healthcare that sucks. It is starting to look a lot like Cuba. Thanks to this incompetent idiot. Yea it's headed in the right direction but the right direction for whom?

I can say one thing for Obama he tells beautiful eloquently worded lies. I just wish he could flap his ears at the same time, now that would be a sight and he could distract the people better from his lies. Well maybe just the Kool aide drinkers. It is a good thing that his ears don't grow with every lie or he would be close to flying.

Obama is not known for being honest. The economy won't really improve until our unemployed have jobs and that can't happen unless our factories are reopened, all jobs farmed out to India and other countries have been returned to the United States, and the illegal aliens, who are costing many billions of taxpayer dollars have been removed from this country. It would also help immensely if the rich paid higher taxes.

I lost all faith, trust, and hope in Obama, when he instructed Geithner and Summers to ask Senator Dodd to sneak language into the Stimulus Bill hours before it was to be voted on, which allowed AIG to give themselves huge bonuses for nearly destroying their company. When the language was discovered after the Bill was voted on, Senator Dodd lied and said that he didn't know how it got there. That's when Obama said that it was his decision to ask Dodd to insert the language into the Bill without giving an honest explanation.

If it were logical and legal, Dodd wouldn't have snuck the language into the Bill and then lied about doing so. And the only reason the Senators didn't do anything about this dishonest act, was that they would have had to admit that they voted on a Bill without reading it.

This act proved to me that Obama was a dishonest man who was extremely greedy, just like most, if not all of the politicians in Washington. I am curious as to the size of the bribes that AIG must have paid to get these folks to do such a blatantly dishonest deed.

If we vote out all of the incumbents who are running in the next election, Congress and the new President just might get the message to do what is good for the country and all the citizens and not their cronies.

Obama's statement that we are moving in the right direction just proves he wants to do us in. You can tell he was never in the service because he's advancing to the rear and thinks it's the right direction. He's living proof that one of the requirements for the presidency should be that the candidate has served in the service. That would take care of a lot of the goofs he has made and save the country from more of same. It's hard to believe that this country actually voted him into office. Our citizenry should be more discriminating.

Two and one half years ago, I constantly called Obama a Marxist radical who is unqualified to be President. I was constantly censored and flamed. My how times have changed? Obama's cash for clunkers program got most of the Obama bumper stickers off the road. The only time you see an Obama sticker is on a Black person's car or a stinking unwashed hippie's car.

Hey guys I do not know about you but I sure would like some of what Obama is taking. The world in his head sure sounds nicer then this one I am living in. Anyways as I was going to say I read the December jobs report but I have to ask are we really going to look at the holiday temporary workers as job creation. How about this we look at the January job creation you know more permanent jobs. Yah ok granted that may not be fair since all the temporary jobs created in December will be going away this month so maybe February jobs will be a better choice.

All he knows for sure is if he can tell enough lies there will be a certain percentage believe him and maybe that will put him over the top voter wise. Maybe there are enough people that want to believe him because they are desperate enough to believe anything that will give them hope to survive. Maybe he will but by God it will not be by my vote.

Obama wants to create more poor people OK? I see why he thinks the economy is moving in the "right" direction. We are definitely creating more poor.

Where does this guy live gas is almost $4 a gallon, and let us not talk about the price of food, thank you Barry, your real smart. The economy is getting worse. No spin is going to change the real truth so guess what we can see, hear, taste, smell and feel the truth.

The only thing that is scarier than Obama is the people that voted for him. That unfortunately is one of the major problems that we face. There are very large numbers of Hispanic, Black and people living on entitlements that will always vote Democratic.

Obama says, "The government will give you this and that and everything else." John F. Kennedy said: "Ask not what your country can do for you, ask what you can do for your country." My, my how the Democratic Party has changed.

The political parties need to start listening to what the citizens of the United States are telling them. It is apparent that a large percentage of Americans are not satisfied with the way the government is performing. When will the government needs to start listening to what the citizens want?

AMERICAN CITIZENS POLITICAL ACTION COMMITTEE WOULD LIKE TO KNOW WHERE ALL OF THE CANDIDATES STAND ON THE ISSUES THAT ARE IN NEED OF LEGISLATION AND ACTION.

IT DOESN'T MATTER WHAT OFFICE THE CANDIDATES ARE RUNNING FOR THEY NEED TO EXPLAIN TO THE CITIZENS WHAT THEY ARE GOING TO BE DOING TO IMPROVE OUR COUNTRY.

WE BELIEVE THAT EVERY CANDIDATE SHOULD BE ABLE TO TELL THE AMERICAN CITIZENS WHAT THEIR POLICY IS GOING TO BE. MORE IMPORTANTLY, HOW THEY PLAN TO EXECUTE THEIR PLANS AND TURN THEM INTO REALITY FOR THE BETTERMENT OF ALL THE CITIZENS OF THE

UNITED STATES OF AMERICA.

The American Citizens Political Action Committee is concerned with the direction that the federal and state governments are taking this country. The government does not have any transparency and the people are not being listened to. It is time that the voting citizens voice their opinions and vote for representation that will vote for programs that are for "We the People, By the People and For the People".

PROGRAM EIGHT:

GETTING AMERICANS JOBS

The American Citizens Political Action Committee will support the politicians that understand that creating American jobs is the most critical piece of legislation that can be passed. It is not the government's job to create jobs but to encourage private businesses to create jobs. However, the government can create programs that can be implemented by private industry that will create jobs.

WORK PROJECTS

A government project that could be implemented quickly would be to complete the southern border fence.

The administration should implement a work project similar to the building of the Hoover Dam. There were unemployed workers from all over the United States that went to Nevada and built the dam. If you have ever been to visit the Hoover Dam you realize just how big a project it was. The result was that the government put thousands of men to work and the benefit was that the dam generates the power for the city of Las Vegas, Nevada and sends power to many other areas. It was a major project that put people to work.

The roughly 1,969 miles of border between the United States and Mexico could be a fantastic work project that many thousands of unemployed Americans would volunteer to work on. With the mass work force the project could be finished in a realistic time frame. Instead of paying the workers unemployment benefits the United States would be benefiting from the security of our border. Anyone that is on unemployment that does not want to work on the border will have their benefits stopped unless they are physically unable to do the work. The area where the fence needs to be built is in an area where the work could be done year around. These would be permanent jobs until the fence is completed.

In addition, there will be thousands of jobs that open up due to the lack of illegals that would have flooded the labor market. The training these men received would help them get into construction jobs upon their return to their homes.

The construction of the fence would only allow American workers and not any illegals or green card holders. This is a save America project. The Army Corps of Engineers could be in charge of the project. The labor cost of the fence would be recovered by the decrease in payments to the unemployed and the reduction of natural resources that are being wasted by the government by supporting the illegals.

The problem is that the current administration apparently does not want the border secure for some unknown reason. The United States has the resources to do the job they just need to want to do the job. It is all political and that just is terrible for the American citizens.

What the current administration is neglecting in the process of not securing the borders is that there may be thousands of terrorists that are crossing with the illegals. Not to mention the amount of drugs that is being smuggled across these unprotected borders. Just what is the Department of Homeland Security thinking about? Suing Arizona?

THE RETURN OF INDUSTRY

The United States is rapidly becoming the very first post industrial nation on the globe. All great economic empires eventually become fat and lazy and squander the great wealth that their forefathers have left them, but the pace at which America is accomplishing this is absolutely amazing. It was America that was at the forefront of the industrial revolution. It was America that showed the world how to mass produce everything from automobiles to televisions to airplanes. It was the great American manufacturing base that crushed Germany and Japan in World War II. But now we are witnessing the deindustrialization of America. Tens of thousands of factories have left the United States in the past decade alone. Millions upon millions of manufacturing jobs have been lost in the same time period. The United States has become a nation that consumes everything in sight and yet produces increasingly little. Do you know what our biggest export is today? Waste paper! Yes, trash is the number one thing that we ship out to the rest of the world as we voraciously blow our money on whatever the rest of the world wants to sell to us. The United States has become bloated and spoiled and our economy is now just a shadow of what it once was. Once upon a time America could literally out produce the rest of the world combined. Today that is no longer true, but Americans sure do consume more than anyone else in the world. If the deindustrialization of America continues at this current pace, what possible kind of a future are we going to be leaving to our children?

Any great nation throughout history has been great at making things. So if the United States continues to allow its manufacturing base to erode at a staggering pace how in the world can the United States continue to consider itself to be a great nation? We have created the biggest debt bubble in the history of the world in an effort to maintain a very high standard of living, but the current state of affairs is not anywhere close to sustainable. Every single month America goes into more debt and every single month America gets poorer. So what happens when the debt bubble pops?

The deindustrialization of the United States should be a top concern for every man, woman and child in the country. But sadly, most Americans do not have any idea what is going on around them. For people like that, take this article and print it out and hand it to them. Perhaps what they will read below will shock them badly enough to awaken them from their slumber. The following are 19 facts about the deindustrialization of America that will blow your mind....

#1 The United States has lost approximately 42,400 factories since 2001.

About 75 percent of those factories employed over 500 people when they were still in operation.

#2 Dell Inc., one of America's largest manufacturers of computers, has announced plans to dramatically expand its operations in China with an investment of over $100 billion over the next decade.

#3 Dell has announced that it will be closing its last large United States manufacturing facility in Winston-Salem, North Carolina in November 2010. Approximately 900 jobs will be lost.

#4 In the year 2008, 1.2 billion cell phones were sold worldwide. So how many of them were manufactured inside the United States? Zero none nada.

#5 According to a new study conducted by the Economic Policy Institute, if the United States trade deficit with China continues to increase at its current rate, the United States economy will lose over half a million jobs this year alone.

#6 At the the of July 2010, the United States trade deficit with China had risen 18 percent compared to the same time period a year ago.

#7 The United States has lost a total of about 5.5 million manufacturing jobs since October 2000.

#8 According to Tax Notes, between 1999 and 2008 employment at the foreign affiliates of United States parent companies increased an astounding 30 percent to 10.1 million. During that exact same time period, United States employment at American multinational corporations declined 8 percent to 21.1 million.

#9 In 1959, manufacturing represented 28 percent of United States economic output. In 2008, it represented 11.5 percent.

#10 Ford Motor Company recently announced the closure of a factory that produces the Ford Ranger in St. Paul, Minnesota. Approximately 750 good paying middle class jobs are going to be lost because making Ford Rangers in Minnesota does not fit in with Ford's new "global" manufacturing strategy.

#11 On December 31, 2009, less than 12 million Americans worked in manufacturing. The last time less than 12 million Americans were employed in manufacturing was in 1941.

#12 In the United States today, consumption accounts for 70 percent of GDP. Of this 70 percent, over half is spent on services.

#13 The United States has lost a whopping 32 percent of its manufacturing jobs since the year 2000.

#14 In 2001, the United States ranked fourth in the world in per capita broadband Internet use. Today it ranks 15th.

#15 The rate of manufacturing employment in the United States computer industry is actually lower in 2010 than it was in 1975.

#16 Printed circuit boards are used in tens of thousands of different products. Asia now produces 84 percent of them worldwide.

#17 The United States spends approximately $3.90 on Chinese goods for every $1 that the Chinese spend on goods from the United States.

#18 One prominent economist is projecting that the Chinese economy will be three times larger than the United States economy by the year 2040.

#19 The United States Census Bureau says that 43.6 million Americans are now living in poverty and according to them that is the highest number of poor Americans in the 51 years that records have been kept.

So how many tens of thousands more factories do we need to lose before we do something about it?

How many millions more Americans are going to become unemployed before we all admit that we have a very, very serious problem on our hands?

How many more trillions of dollars are going to leave the country before we realize that we are losing wealth at a pace that is killing our economy?

How many once great manufacturing cities are going to become rotting war zones like Detroit before we understand that we are committing national economic suicide?

The deindustrialization of America is a national crisis. It needs to be treated like one.

America is in deep, deep trouble folks. It is past time to wake up.

It is only a matter of time until our currency will be totally worthless. Unless your stocks are in international companies, they will be devalued also. The price of commodities, precious metals, industrial metals, copper, tin, aluminum, etc., will continue to increase with the price of energy and food. Once the collapse begins, if anarchy doesn't rule, it will take ten years or more to begin to dig out of the mess and try to rebuild America. Will you have the resources to weather the drought period? There could be untold riches awaiting those who prepare now. But it takes money to make money. Be sure you are holding something of value when the dollar takes a nose dive. And pray we are able to maintain a first class military. We will need it when China and Russia combine to form the largest and most modernized military ever imagined. In twenty years China will be able to outspend us three to one on military expenditures. I am sure they wish us the best of health.

DOUBLE DIPPING

That's why stories of $195,000 pensions, rampant double-dipping, workers collecting pensions on seven, eight or even nine government jobs, and other excesses seem so absurd. And pension gamesmanship is routine around the country. For example, pension payments are often based on the employee's salary in the final year on the job, or final three years. That formula is easily abused, a process sometimes called "back-ending." A pension commission in New Jersey found one worker spent 24 years in public service earning less than $10,000, then one year as a prosecutor earning $141,000. That boosted his pension from $3,600 to $70,000 annually. The employee wasn't named.

There are probably as many variations as you can imagine. Just when we think that we've heard something amazing, I'll hear something more amazing. It goes on everywhere across the country. It's human nature; if you can figure out a way to inflate your pension, you are going to do it. People who make a career of it are making out like bandits.

Another common pension abuse is "double-dipping" – a practice in which employees retire and start collecting their pension, and then they are rehired to perform their old job at their old salary. It's a common practice for government workers around the country, despite many rules forbidding it. Workers often argue that they have earned their pension and their right to retire, and if they decide to work during retirement, they're entitled. But the logic there is deeply flawed.

Pensions were designed to make sure government workers were allowed to grow old with dignity, not to make them rich.

In this series on super-sized government pay, we've already met Phoenix police chief/public safety manager Jack Harris, who's become the nation's poster child for "double-dipping." He retired as chief in 2007 and began collecting a $90,000 pension. Two weeks later, he was hired for essentially the same job, re-titled "public safety manager," and granted a salary of $193,000. Harris attracted nationwide attention after a lawsuit was filed by conservative interest group Judicial Watch. The lawsuit claims the public safety manager's job was manufactured expressly to circumvent both pension rules and a state law aimed at curbing the practice.

Peter Tom is a municipal compensation specialist who's worked in New Jersey's complicated government worker environment for three decades. New Jersey even has rules designed to enable double-dippers, he said. Yet, he's seen all manner of pension-stuffing through the years.

This would not be allowed in the private sector because the pension committees are third party administrators who have fiduciary responsibilities.

While the outrage factor on six-figure pensions and lucrative loopholes is high, there is a more practical, actuarial problem: Pension recipients aren't paying their fair share, creating unfunded liabilities. For example, a worker who pays 5 percent of a $10,000 salary into the system for 24 years, then 5 percent of a $140,000 salary for one year, doesn't cover the costs of a $70,000 pension.

These loopholes create unfunded liabilities that have helped damage the pension pool. Pensioners are never asked to make up the difference.

In truth, pension systems rely on what might be considered an accounting trick, not unlike the trick which keeps the Social Security system afloat for now. While state workers contribute payments to the system – typically about 5 percent of their salary -- and those payments are matched by government employers -- about 10 percent -- those payments scarcely cover the eventual payouts. You can never pay enough to pay for your retirement.

In fact, "defined benefit" pension plans make no direct connection between the worker's contributions and the benefits enjoyed later. Pension systems hope for large investment gains during a worker's career – in many states the calculations project an annual return of around 8 percent, a fantasy -- but really rely on the payments of current workers to fund payouts to retired workers.

Just as pensions are a bit of an accounting trick (or a Ponzi scheme, some might argue), pension obligations do not appear on state balance sheets as debts. If they did – if states actually had to write down what they owe retirees going forward, and assume a modest return on investments -- the unfunded portion of the payments could be as high as $4.3 trillion. That's nearly a third of the federal debt, which currently stands at $13.7 trillion. The federal government's massive debt steals headlines, vaults politicians to office and has its own Times Square clock, but at least Washington, D.C., can print money. Meanwhile, states are staring at a huge mammoth black hole with seemingly no way to dig out.

While the contribution formulas have systematic flaws, their shortcomings are severely exacerbated by another simple math problem – life expectancy has jumped almost 10 years since 1960.

Unions managed to lower or reduce the retirement age while increasing benefits in a period of history where people are living longer. So you begin seeing what the problem is.

There is a police chief who will pull in $5 million in California before he is projected to die.

Most pension reformers are calling for state governments to switch to a defined contribution system, similar to 401(k) plans many workers have. That would mean workers would only get what they put into the system -- combined with any employer cash contributions and supplemented by investment gains -- when they retire.

But while that is fiscally responsible from the government's point of view, a defined contribution plan is a meager replacement for a defined benefit plan. That's why unions are putting up quite a fight against pension reform.

Here's a simple rule-of-thumb comparison. A 30-year government worker with a final salary of $80,000 could expect an annual pension of roughly $55,000, or about $4,600 per month for life, under the current scheme.

To earn that kind of guaranteed monthly income, a 401(k) saver would need $1 million in their retirement account, assuming $100,000 in savings can generate $400 in monthly income.

While it's not impossible to grow a 401(k) to those lofty levels, it is rare. In fact, 50 percent of Americans who have 401(k) accounts have less than $35,000 in them. Contrast that with our 30-year government workers who can all expect predictable pension checks.

So expect a furious battle as state governments attempt to reign in pension costs.

But in the end, pensions are about power. Elected officials from local and state governments maintain power by doling out favors and perks, and there is no perk like a pension.

The governments need to enact legislation that the employee that is double dipping is removed from their current job. We have

unemployment reported by the government of 9.8% in the United States. The real number of people unemployed is more like 20% when you consider all those that have decided to quit looking for work and those that have used up all of their benefits.

These double dipping employees should be required to resign so that the younger generation of employees can be hired to fill the positions that are being occupied by the double dippers. This will provide for two things. First, it will reduce the government payrolls by letting newer employees enter the market at lower pay rates than the double dippers. Second, it will allow the government to reduce the number of employees due to the fact that they would only have to replace the ones that are actually required to be functional. We need for the government to reduce the size of the work force by at least 20 – 25 percent. There is at least that much waste in the governments operations.

The detection of the double dippers will be very easy to accomplish. Every employee that files an income tax return that reports retirement income and received a Form 1099 could be detected. When they file a return that has a W-2 from current government employment as well they would have their name placed into a data bank. If they do not voluntarily resign the government could release them with cause and fine them $25,000. The fine will deter these employees from double dipping. This will make every union member scream bloody murder.

The other part of the problem is the governments needing to be union controlled. If the government is such a great place to work, why are the unions needed anyway?

REPLACING ILLEGALS WITH AMERICANS

When the federal government starts to enforce the laws regarding the illegal problem in the United States we will be able to replace approximately 12,000,000 illegals that are currently working in the United States with American workers. The unemployment rate will go down to levels that are acceptable and the government will realize a substantial increase in the revenue from these American workers.

To keep the numbers simple, we will use an annual income of $20,000 per illegal. We know that they are more than likely being paid in cash so the government will not receive the social security and Medicare payments that would normally be deducted and matched by the employer. That would work out to the illegals being paid $240 billion per year. The payroll tax deductions would provide the government with over $25 billion per year. Another benefit would be that the $25 billion to $40 billion that the illegals send back to Mexico every year would stay in the economy of the United States of America. Then there would be major benefits of removing these illegal workers out of the entitlement programs.

This problem creates so many benefits for the United States that it is unimaginable that our government does not want to do anything about deporting the illegals and improving the lives of the American Citizens.

REPEALING THE NAFTA

The North American Free Trade Agreement (NAFTA) should be abolished between the United States and Mexico. The simple facts are that Mexico has declared war against the United States with their invasion of 20 million illegals that have entered into the United States. Although it has not been a military invasion it is definitely taking our resources and the quality of life from the citizens of the United States.

The United States needs to stop doing business with the Mexican's until such a time as the borders are secure and the illegals that are residing in the country are returned.

We the people of the United States need to practice self discipline and cancel all travel plans that include stops in any part of Mexico. Mexico needs to lose out on all of the American tourist money. We have an abundance of beautiful places in the United States that everyone could use to enjoy on their vacations. Why not go to Hawaii or Alaska instead? We need to return to our roots and enjoy America the Beautiful. For those of you who want to see what it is like in Mexico travel to Southern California.

The United States has lost over one million jobs since NAFTA began in January 1994. The value added tax is one of the most negative economic games that are played on the consumer. Don't kid yourself every country has a value added tax to their imports except America. These value added taxes are one of the primary reasons that American companies ship their jobs out of the United States. They can use cheap labor to produce overly cheap products in a foreign country and ship the manufactured products back to America free of a value added tax. There go our American manufacturing jobs to another country and up goes our unemployment rate.

The United States needs to incorporate a value added tax on all merchandise that comes into the country and protect our manufacturing base and put every company on an equal basis. When everything becomes equal the manufacturing will return to the United States and our economy will start to revive.

The federal government is borrowing trillions of dollars to keep our economy running. Something is seriously wrong and our economic priorities are up side down. The economy can not be restarted from the government. It has to be started from the local communities by creating new jobs and saving our housing.

PROGRAM NINE:

NO AMNESTY FOR ANYONE

With the Republicans taking control of the House and representing a stronger minority in the Senate next year, failure to enact the legislation by year's end dims the prospects for action by Congress to grant a path toward legalization for the nation's millions of undocumented immigrants.

Tamar Jacoby of Immigration Works USA, a pro-immigration employer's coalition, said the defeat won't end Congress' attempts to address the issue but predicted that future legislation will look far different. "Anything that they're going to do is going to disappoint comprehensive immigration reform advocates," Jacoby said. "It's going to be a tough haul" to tackle the subject in the new Congress.

After the House vote, Obama issued a statement pledging to move forward on immigration reform and casting the Dream Act as a way of correcting what he called "one of the most egregious flaws of a badly broken immigration system."

Every American needs to contact their representatives in Congress and make sure that there will not be any legislation that will give amnesty to any illegal. When are the Democrats going to listen to what America wants with regard to amnesty? The Democrats do not listen to anything else for that matter that the people want.

The citizens of the United States need to make sure that their representatives in Congress understand that the American people do not want any kind of amnesty for any illegal that is in the United States. Every illegal needs to be deported without exception. The Congress needs to step up and face the problems that are being caused by the 20 million illegals that are currently in the United States.

These are uncut and from all over the United States. They should display to the politicians what the citizens of the United States feel about any form of amnesty. They also make statements about securing our borders to stop the flow of the illegals into the United States.

Bring the troops home from Afghanistan and Iraq and it will be far cheaper to feed, arm and direct them on our own borders. They are equipped, trained and able to defend the United States Border and that is what they should be doing. Let the camel jockeys kill each other off and if necessary France, Germany and Italy can finish off the last one standing. This nation is being economically gutted by the illegals in our factories, farms, hospitals, schools and welfare offices. Give them notice unhampered passage home to celebrate their holidays and don't come back. The rest should leave within 60 days or be hunted down and marched across the border. We will take our jobs back--without SEIU, Teamsters, or other union representation. Union workers, you want your jobs back, get rid of the unions that Obama is selling out to.

Arizona has the right attitude -- enforce the laws. We can't take care of our own citizens with jobs availability and yet we want to give illegals the right to take what jobs are available from the USA very own citizens.

Don't extend the unemployment benefits free gratis; make them do something for those dollars. There are a lot of streets needing cleaned, debris pick up; volunteering at shelters, etc. Why would anyone actively look for work when they get a pay check to sit at home, not have to worry about clothing, gas, baby sitters, etc? They are further ahead to sit on their butts and let the rest of us take care of them. Granted this isn't all of them.

Stop suing states for enforcing immigration laws; start enforcing laws everywhere. Let those here who want citizenship earn that right; same as anyone else coming into the states. We don't need more welfare and more handouts for the illegals. Making them citizens won't change that problem. Also, when these young people are given citizenship, then their parents, grandparents, aunts, uncles, cousins, etc can come in. Where is this nation's sanity? Forget the votes; work for the people.

How does granting amnesty and citizenship to illegals help increase our national security?

How about finally securing our southern borders and actually enforcing Federal laws already on the books when they're caught? Not much has been done that's effective, even though it's almost 10 years after 9/11/2001.

Won't that dramatically increase national security? Wasn't this also supposed to happen when President Reagan granted amnesty to millions of illegals? All that did was increase the flow of illegals heading north.

I don't have a soft spot in my heart for children illegally in the United States. Not when our own children who are citizens may suffer from supporting illegals or 'anchor babies', and not where such humanitarian aid doesn't seem to affect the world view of the United States anyway.

Sounds like the fascist Democrats are trying to break the system even more. If they are illegal they should be deported. No one that came into this country illegally should be allowed to be a citizen. This bill makes a mockery of the law.

I should hope to shout. Illegal is illegal. Try this stunt in any other country in the world and you get put in jail, (and in some you get shot), get deported, etc. Only in America can you come in illegally, live off the backs of working people, get government aid and then demand citizenship. Let's use the last part of the word and "ship" them back where they came from. Let them come in the front door, learn our language and customs, and become legal citizens.

It seems strange that the American taxpayers pay these senators salary but all they want to do is support the illegals. Time for many of these folks to go home, retire or get beat. It's sad that Reid and Pelosi are still with us since both of them should have been booted.

Has any one of these Senators heard the voice of the people? No, just pandering for the illegal votes. Remember, Reid, it was the Hispanics that put you into office. Another point I must make, you work for the American citizens, We the People do not work for you. There shouldn't be any amnesty for any illegals.

"Comprehensive immigration reform" amnesty would initiate Chain Migration of even more by illegals who often have little desire in assimilation or family planning and potentially erode the culture and sovereignty of this great nation.

Some say "it is impossible to deport 20 million illegals. Actually, the first 50 % would be easy to locate. But, there is an easier way to do it. Fine and jail the landlords and employers that have hired the illegals and provided them a place to live. Terminate all taxpayer funded public services to illegals as allowed by the constitution.

Then the illegals will use the "Feet don't fail me now" program. Self deportation will happen and recent economic history and current events in Arizona have shown "Feet don't fail me now" works. The same way they came here is the same way they can go home. This would provide an effective and taxpayer friendly way for illegals to deport themselves.

Totally agree. As a society, we already recognize that people should not benefit from operating an illegal enterprise (drug dealers). When we catch and convict them, we confiscate all of their assets. Those who employ illegals...and the illegals themselves....are operating illegal enterprises. We should treat them the same way as the drug dealers.

We don't sell American citizenship or pay for you to go to college so you get it for free. If the staffing for the military is needed, re-install the draft and reward our citizens for their service. As for as the Hispanic activists groups is concerned, their interest is not the United States but rewarding people from other nations, expecting us to pay for it, so screw them.

My daughter was not able to get any help for college because she was not: Hispanic, African American, Pregnant, did not have kids, did not live on the streets. She lived at home, worked 35-40 hours a week and went to school full time. She was not able to get any help. But if you are an illegal you get welfare, food stamps and a free education. What happened to those who help themselves gain success? Oh I forgot under our new socialist Democratic government working hard, making money and becoming wealthy is a bad thing to do so the government will take your hard earned money and give to some lazy slob so he can be happy. That is not a great way to treat the people that have worked hard to better themselves.

If this dream act, or any form of it is passed the "People of the USA" must demand that the President and any member of Congress resign, or be charged with treason. Illegals have spit on our laws and we can't afford this, and no where else in the World is this tolerated. The President and members of Congress need to get this through their thick sculls.

Sneaking into this country = illegal

Having a passport without entry stamp = illegal

Working without a permit = illegal

Knowingly employing an illegal = illegal

Not paying taxes = illegal

Working and using fake ID = illegal + illegal

Working using your legal friend's ID = illegal

Driving with fake or borrowed ID = illegal

Driving with fake ID insurance = illegal

Living 30 to a 1 bedroom apartment = illegal

Reproducing and having a baby on US welfare = illegal

Sending your litter of kids to US schools = illegal

Protesting in the USA = illegal

An act of terrorism = illegal

An act of anarchy against the USA – illegal

If you put this issue to a national referendum...and be diligent in not allowing illegals to vote, as the Democrats have locally made it possible to do in so many places, this idea of fast tracking citizenship would be voted down by the electorate in huge numbers. It would probably be the one, true bipartisan issue since WWII that would be soundly defeated. The Democrats, Republicans, Independents, Blacks, Whites, legal Hispanics, Christians, Muslims, Atheists and Jews would support the legislation. All people who believe in fairness, respect for law, respect for society and culture, respect for doing the right thing, who loudly say no. We have legal ways to enter and stay. To reward people who have come here illegally simply isn't right.

Any of us get caught doing something illegal we get the book thrown at us. Why is it that illegals entering our country get the red carpet treatment? Quit offering illegals a better life. Seal the borders shoot a few trying to swim the big river and that should at least start a word of mouth rumor that the party is over. You can't stop a problem when you keep giving them a good reason to come here illegally!

The Democrats really do not care about the immigrants. They see them as nothing but slam dunk votes and tilting the social scales in their direction of power. They have the black vote by providing social programs but has the black population really done better? The truthful answer is both yes and no. Yes, because they do it themselves and no because they wait on the government. The Democrats will line buses up to get you to the voting booths but not a single bus to get you back across the border. Wake up, the Government is not the answer it is the problem.

Calling an illegal alien an 'undocumented immigrant' is like calling a drug dealer an 'unlicensed pharmacist.'

How about the illegals make an effort to act like they can even follow laws before they demand legal status? They don't seem to understand that by the very fact that they crossed the border illegally that they are criminals. They need to speak English before they demand rights and privileges that are due to citizens. Better yet they need to pack up and leave...and all the liberals who support them need to shut up or leave with them.

The government wouldn't help out with my son's college tuition at all, not one penny. So he is now not going to college but working to save for school. I haven't got much money. I am a white guy born in the United States of America and I have always paid taxes and I have worked my whole life. And I watch as illegal aliens waltz in here to get subsidized by our tax dollars to get a degree. This is just disgusting. What have the liberals done to our country?

This is a general comment on illegal immigration. I live in South Texas, 10 miles from the border. I can guarantee you that I associate with more illegals in a day than most of you do in a year. I know these people. And for the record, I'm white. These people aren't doctors, engineers, scientists and they certainly don't want to enlist in the military. The jobs they get are fast food workers, janitors, landscapers, construction workers, mechanics and farm workers. If every single illegal was deported tomorrow, the worst that would happen is the price of your head of lettuce would go up by a dollar, or you might have to pay a bit more for your lawn to be fertilized. The idea that illegals are good for our economy is demonstrably wrong. It's been proven that 56% of illegal families are on some form of public assistance. Illegal immigration is wrong, and needs to be stopped NOW.

I am confused. How it is that illegals are allowed to attend our public schools? The public schools financed by our tax dollars. What type of precedent does it set when our government and law enforcement agencies turn a blind eye to the laws of our nation and refuse to enforce them? Perhaps we could all simply find a law we do not care for and openly and defiantly disobey it? Probably not however, but why I am not sure.

Now they want to surrender our sovereignty to a foreign power under the guise of "immigration reform". That means putting all of Mexico on America's welfare rolls. Thank the Hispanic congressional caucus. What are you selling next time cancer?

Are we all crazy here, or what? Give the children of illegals a leg up over our own kids to get into college? They will take the place of taxpaying citizens' kids in our state schools, and probably get tuition assistance as well, because they will probably be from low income families. This is truly beyond belief. Harry Reid needs to be horsewhipped. And the media said his opponent, Sharon angle, was crazy?

Fathom the odd hypocrisy that Obama wants every citizen to prove they are insured, but on the other hand, people don't have to prove they are citizens". Now, isn't that something!

Now we got thousands of Americans who fought in the Mexican war that is spinning in their graves at the sheer lunacy of our government and its hidden agenda of merging our country with Mexico. Thanks to our government we are now fast becoming a third world country or banana republic with rampant crime, drugs, low quality of life, near insolvent states, high cost of living, tax dollars going to subsidize immigrants with welfare, health care and a myriad of other problems. Thanks to a government that only cares about perpetuating its own existence

We've seen how these illegal kids think of themselves as being "American" here in Houston. When they protest their status in high schools, they go out and raise the Mexican flag. The idea that they consider themselves anything but Mexican is absurd. How naive do these leftist liberals and Hispanic activists (make that Hispanic nationalists) think we are.

We have neighborhoods and complete subdivisions loaded with weed-growing nose snuffing illegals. They pack three or four families to a house and live like scared gophers. They drive without licenses steal from stores and live like pigs in a barn yard.

I believe that the message is clear from Americans that we will not tolerate any form of amnesty. It will start a real revolt in this country and is not what Americans want. How come the President and Congress can not understand what the citizens America want and act accordingly?

PROGRAM TEN:

THE UNITED STATES DECLINING ECOMOMY

The American Citizens Political Action Committee is pleased to present the thoughts of the citizens of the United States. When you read the comments it will make you wonder why the representatives in Congress and the President are not able to see the problems that are facing the country. When will the President and Congress start listening to what the people are concerned about instead of looking out for their next vote? Why don't they understand that when they start listening to the people they will not have to worry about being re-elected because they will be doing their jobs properly?

The following article is presented to help the American people understand the problem of our economy. The government needs to pass legislation to curtail the amount of our trade deficit. We need to reduce the amount of junk products that are produced in China and the rest of the Asian countries. The United States needs to start manufacturing these products and return our workforce to the employed. Our country was made famous by the Americans buying the products that were "Made in USA" we have to start buying our products instead of the foreign countries products.

Economists foretell of United States decline and China's ascension

By Mark Felsenthal – Mon Jan 10, 2011

DENVER (Reuters) – To hear a number of prominent economists tell it, it doesn't look good for the U.S. economy, not this year, not in 10 years.

Leading thinkers in the dismal science speaking at an annual convention offered varying visions of U.S. economic decline, in the short, medium and long term. This year, the recovery may bog down as government stimulus measures dry up.

In the long run, the United States must face up to inevitably being overtaken by China as the world's largest economy. And it may have missed a chance to rein in its largest financial institutions, many of whom remain too big to fail and are getting bigger.

On the one hand, Harvard's Martin Feldstein said he believes the outlook for U.S. economic growth in 2011 is less sanguine than many believe.

First, the boost to growth from government spending will be drying up this year, he said. Renewal of expiring tax cuts is no more than a decision not to raise taxes, and the impact of one-year payroll tax cut is likely modest, he said.

"There's really not much help coming from fiscal policy in the year ahead," he said. Woes from the dire situations of state and local governments may actually be a drag on growth, he said.

Growth got a lift from a lower saving rate in 2010, but that probably will not last this year as households worried about an uncertain future return to paring back debt and socking more away, Feldstein added. Discouraging declines in home values mean there is less to save from, he said.

"People are worried, so there's a strong reason for precautionary saving," he said.

THE RACE IS ON

On the other hand, there is the race with China and the dynamic Asian economies, including India. Most estimates put the size of the Chinese economy on par with the United States by the early 2020s, said Dale Jorgenson, also of Harvard.

Jorgenson sees Asian emerging markets as the most dynamic in the world, eclipsing other emerging market contenders such as Brazil and Russia with steady growth over the next decade.

"The rise of developing Asia is going to accompany slower world economic growth," he said.

The United States will need to come to terms with the fact that its prevalence in the world is fated to come to an end, Jorgenson said. This will be difficult for many Americans to swallow and the United States should brace for social unrest amid blame over who was responsible for squandering global primacy, he said.

MIT's Simon Johnson put it more bluntly, saying the damage from the financial crisis and its aftermath have dealt U.S. prominence a permanent blow.

"The age of American predominance is over," he told a panel. "The (Chinese) Yuan will be the world's reserve currency within two decades."

Johnson said he believes the United States has failed to learn its lesson from the financial crisis and continues to implicitly back its largest financial institutions.

"I'm concerned about the excessive power of the largest global banks," he said. "Who are the government-sponsored enterprises now? It's the six biggest bank holding companies."

To be sure, Raghuram Rajan, a former IMF chief economist now with the University of Chicago's Booth School of Business, could still envision an ongoing U.S. leadership role.

Nothing proceeds in a straight line, he said, and there are many pitfalls along the way even for dynamic Asian economies.

"I would say the age of American dominance may be nearing an end. But America as the biggest mover will be in place for a long time," he said.

(Reporting by Mark Felsenthal; Editing by Maureen Bavdek)

What the supporters of the American Citizens Political Action Committee think about the above article and the condition of the United States of America. The Committee will present some possible solutions to the problem after we read the comments.

Blame for the decline in the American economy and America's position in the world can only be laid onto the American people. It is all of us who decide to buy that cheaper priced (made in China) product when we shop that not only contributes to China's ascension but to our decline as well. It's a double-whammy when you buy something Made in China. Think about it?

We are rapidly becoming a third world country with a shrinking

middle class who must work ever longer and harder to be able to pay for the free housing, food, education and health care of the minorities and the illegals. We have become a country whose rising population is mostly those who survive on handouts. On the other end, we are more and more seeing our government's policies being developed for the good of the elite and big corporations. Wall Street is doing fine, so are the illegals and the minorities, and just how are all of you in the middle class doing?

What I don't understand is: Won't Asia continues to gentrify and won't that drive up the cost of their goods? Won't rising oil prices make manufacturing at home more lucrative (ships need diesel)? If the United States starts buying less Chinese goods what will happen to their future markets? Economies are complicated folks. The standard of living might dip, but the quality of life may get better. Americans need to cool it on the national freak out and work hard and have a little imagination.

Our government has been in bed with big business for a long long time. It has not mattered which party was in control of the Congress. President Bush Sr. started GATT/NAFTA; Clinton with the help of Al Gore's deciding vote passed NAFTA in a fast-track voting procedure, Bush Jr. then pushed even more jobs out of the country as United States workers took fake jobs created from the housing boom. When the dust cleared and the real jobs had been shipped out of the country...there was nothing left...just this ruined economy? Derivatives and stock scams plagued since the Clinton Days. Bush Sr. had the Savings and Loan scams, Clinton stock bubble scams and Bush Jr. debt swaps and derivatives. It's easy to see greed killed the United States of America and you can thank Summers, Ruben and Greenspan too!

The majority of the people in the United States are welfare leaches. $100,000 a year government pensions included. My former Union President famous quote "the future of the Union is nobody doing any work!" The plant closed, it is now an empty field. As long as that mentality reins from the top of the government to the homeless street bum this country is headed into the sewer.

If all economists were laid end to end, they would not reach a conclusion. George Bernard Shaw

WHO TO BLAME?

The answer is easy. Ourselves we bought into a marketed version of the American Dream, cheap credit, and materialistic being. The American Dream of people like Jefferson was about equality, happiness, security, and modest wealth. It is been bought, sold, and contrived into 'wealth above all else' and "keeping up with the Jones". We have built our economy over the last 2 decades on speculative lending, cheap credit, and over inflated sense of value. Calling a house a $500,000 house, does not, in reality, make it a $500,000 house.

We've forgotten how to produce our own goods, we've forgotten how to buy locally, and we've shipped our wealth all over the globe for cheap oil and cheap goods. We are not a production nation, our main 'goods' are services...and you can't support an economy simply on services.

We believed in "we're #1 and USA USA USA". We got complacent and failed to understand the simple writing on the wall. 308,750,000 Americans aren't going to out produce a nation of 1.2 billion.

Oh, I suppose it doesn't help that in our efforts to pursue and push the American way, we've done a good job of losing our moral authority. We played the role of the bully many times and we can only hope that when the tide turns that China and Russia (Russia will be China's #1 partner, not us) allow us to live our lives as we see fit and not push their agenda's on us. Good luck.

But I suppose it's not all bad. Maybe not being the World's superpower will allow us to become a great nation of modest wealth, happiness, and freedom without have to worry about being the world's law enforcement agency. But I suppose we'll have to pay off China first, and somehow deal with the political fallout and social unrest. Best of luck!

With the free trade agreement, and allowing all the United States companies to migrate to other countries all in the name of the almighty dollar, its no wonder this could be happening. Couple that with the favoritism shown to illegals the combination will be the ruin of a great nation. Its time we go back to basics, keep American companies at home, keep illegals out, and look out for Americans first.

The United States has too much government, a system to encourage and reward the lazy do nothing. Instead of rewarding the hard working We reward government workers with $100,000 pensions that retire at 55 and then gets another government job to double dip our economy while the hard working engineer is lucky to have a $100,000 salary and zero pension. Time for a flat tax, cut the size of government in half and spend education money on the smart and not the dumb. Currently any kid with serious problems and doesn't speak English get a one on one "helper". Where as the brightest are lucky to get a special class to really push their brilliance. The fat and lazy get rewarded and the United States of America will continue to decline.

BOYCOTT WALMART

Every American should boycott Wal-Mart until they return to "Made in the USA." The following information should wake up America and show why America needs to wean itself from China.

The Emma Maersk is part of a Danish shipping line that is transporting all of the goods from China to the United States.

What a ship the Emma Maersk is. No wonder "Made in China" is displacing North American made goods big time. This monster transports goods across the Pacific in just 5 days!! This is one of three ships presently in service, with another two ships commissioned to be completed in 2012.

These ships were commissioned by Wal-Mart to get all their goods and stuff from China. They hold an incredible 15,000 cartons and have a 207 foot deck beam!! The full crew is just 13 people on a ship longer than a United States Aircraft Carrier (which has a crew of 5,000) with its 207' beam it is too big to fit through the Panama or Suez Canals.

It is strictly transpacific. Cruise speed: 31 knots.

The goods arrive 4 days before the typical container ship (18-20 knots) on a China to California run. 91% of Wal-Mart products are made in

China. So this behemoth is hugely competitive even when carrying perishable goods.

The ship was built in five sections. The sections floated together then welded.

The command bridge is higher than a 10-story building and has 11 cargo crane rigs that can operate simultaneously unloading the entire ship in less than two hours.

ADDITIONAL INFORMATION:

Country of origin - Denmark

Length - 1,302 feet

Width - 207 feet

Net cargo - 123,200 tons

Engine - 14 cylinders in-line diesel engine generating 110,000 BHP

Cruise Speed - 31 knots

Cargo capacity - 15,000 TEU (1 TEU = 20 cubic feet)

Crew - 13 people

First Trip - Sept. 08, 2006

Construction cost - US $145,000,000 plus

Silicone painting applied to the ship bottom reduces water resistance and saves 317,000 gallons of diesel per year.

A recent documentary in late March, 2010 on the History Channel noted that all of these containers are shipped back to China, <u>EMPTY</u>. Yep, that's right. We send nothing back on these ships. What does that tell you about the current financial state of this country? Just keep buying those imported goods (mostly gadgets) until you run out of money. Then you may wonder what the cause of unemployment (maybe even <u>your</u> job) in the United States might be? Do we need to show you anything more to want you to stop purchasing that junk that is imported from China? Buy products that are "Made in the USA."

Communist China has been one of the greatest concerns for decades to America and yet for decades, we have been giving them economic strength and power by giving them our manufacturing. Sure they wouldn't be able to take out America militarily so they do it (with our capitalist approval) through the side entrance and do it through economic domination. The successful strategy of the Chinese government will let them win without firing a shot.

The writing has been on the wall for over the past 40 years, the wage discrepancy in this country has clearly demonstrated where the goals of the power brokers are, and to what lengths they will go to preserve the status quo.

There are several solutions to the economic problems facing the United States that all should be put in place. First and foremost, American needs to return to being an industrial manufacturing giant and this can be done by reducing the financial burden of running a business in the United States. Reduce the taxes that soak up capital, reduce the environmental regulations that are choking development or tax incentives to invest in advanced technology or methods that reduces pollutants. Unions need to pull back on driving wages to uncompetitive heights just because they can, a living wage yes, but automobile workers do not require $50.00 per hour to baby sit a computer controlled robot assembly machine. Jobs need to be returned to the United States and the fastest way to do that is to tax everything being imported into the United States to be assembled here. Made in America should actually mean MADE IN AMERICA, require everything with that label to have a minimum of 80% of all materials and parts actually be made in America.

Finally, to help the economy and prevent the melt down we suffered because banks and businesses were "TOO BIG TO FAIL", break them up under the Anti Trust Acts. Any Business that is "To Big to Fail" is a monopoly that should be broken up. That would prevent the centralization and concentration of wealth and manufacturing that has lead us to this point. Hell Chase Manhattan, Goldman Sachs and others that were "BAILED OUT" simply took that money and bought out their competition that had remained solvent and did not require a bail out. In other words, the American citizens paid for incompetent banks getting even bigger and an even larger threat to the economy.

In general, this started when we accepted the idea of an open market. We removed protections for American goods and allowed imports of foreign goods with little tariff or tax. This, of course, can't work as foreign workers often work for pennies on the dollar. It means they can produce cheaper goods that we can't compete with. Unless we are willing to go with slave labor, we need to start charging imports and we need to start investing in our own manufacturing base again. Economic policies need to be adjusted to require American companies to manufacture at home again rather than abroad. The time has come to reinvest Americans money in America again.

China needs the people of this country to buy their products to become a world power. All their people's dreams of wealth and power will stop if we in this country stop buying their exported junk.

In order for the United States economy to be good we must have manufactured goods not imported. We have all these geniuses in Washington with no common sense.

A friend of mine, an engineer, has been traveling to China since the early 1980's. He told me of trips to a small manufacturing plant an hour outside of Shanghai. Within 15 minutes of leaving the airport you were out in the rice paddies. Rice farmers would dry their rice on the one road that passed through their farmland. Flash forward 25 years, and the manufacturing plant is 2,500 acres and the rice paddies are gone, replaced by high rise buildings and manufacturing facilities. The entire hour drive is now 3 to 4 hours because of traffic congestion. China's economy will be larger than America's in less than 10 years. One thing that would put a stick in that expansion, would be to resource manufacturing back to America, and impose either quotas, or tariffs, or a combination of both on any manufactured good, from any country. That would cause massive disruption of China's manufacturing sector. Massive job losses and massive civil unrest would follow. It's time that our government was more concerned about jobs in America, instead of paying lips service, and taking campaign contributions from a few thousand very wealthy and influential business Chief Executive Officers and the banking industry.

This is perhaps the 'best information' printed that is clear and direct. People have been saying this for the past 4 decades. Now it seems that it is actually coming to light. The worst part is perhaps, that The American Education Institutions and Business' since the 1970's have taught these countries just how to beat the American Industries. The schools have become day care centers with little emphasis on teaching tomorrows needs. Students find on a day to day basis that education has become outdated before they even graduate. Education standards and reforms need to act upon today's problems and not tomorrow, but should have been done yesterday.

China, India, SE Asia, while Latin America and Western Europe plays a smaller role will be the main stay of the United States Market (Stock Markets). The industries that once allowed the American people to flourish and grow have now become the outsourced factories and businesses across the Oceans. Over 50 percent of all United States manufacturing firms outsource to these parts of the World. Over 65 percent of all IT is outsourced that used to be in Silicon Valley alone. Manufacturing went to China, software going to India, SE Asia and parts of Europe.

Our Congress has allowed those to remove the industries and jobs from the United States while continuing to fill their pockets with profits. Our Government has given away the next two generations of hope by allowing for the banks and corporations to receive trillions of dollars in so-called stimulus that only increases their own power and wealth.

The Stock Market will continue to rise as unemployment and American business disappear. The banks and corporate America will continue to grow as the American public continues to see their production and growth decline. If Congress does not act soon, it will be too late for America to regain or even be able to compete with other nations.

I can remember a few years ago when Wal-Mart had huge banners at the entrances to their stores stating that their blenders were made in Podunk, Arkansas and had created 68 jobs. Funny, those banners are not there anymore. My 7 year old son approached the local Wal-Mart store and notice that there was not a Chinese flag flying on top of the building. He questioned why since all the products were made in China? It is too bad our government does not have that much foresight.

We were told thirty, forty, fifty years ago that if we don't change the way we're doing things this would happen, now the time is here. Conservative religious and political leaders warned us what was coming. With the spending policies, abortion, the gay issue, corruption in government and greed in the privet sector. Then the government steps in and tries to fix it, it's like telling the wolf to fix the broken boards on the hen house. There are other complex problems, but we can't even get the basics right. It sounds simplistic, but it's all connected. Some laugh, but I can't believe it's happening myself, it's obvious even to the most casual observer. Quiet possibly the end is near. Washington is panicking, you can tell by the policies that are being put in place, It won't be long before we start to hear about gun control again, a definite sign Washington is panicking. Just observe what is happening in Washington, actions are also worth a thousand words. Wake up America.

I believe this. But we need stronger leadership from our politicians. Not cradling our big business. And we need to manufacture things in this country.

We also know one of the issues that United States economy is declining day by day is due to outsourcing manufacturing base to China. Why the wealthy is so greedy and let our people (working class) suffer? Almost all of our manufacturing jobs are gone to China. We are spending and using the products and not making much of anything now. We are the country of immigrants and we should keep America strong. Why are the wealthy not thinking of the working class in USA?

America needs to wake up. When we return the manufacturing jobs to America the trend will reverse. Until that time you can only blame yourself for the decline in the status of the United States. Doesn't anyone remember the labels that said: "Made in USA"? Another major problem that the United States is facing is the number of illegals that are in the United States that really do not care if we become a third world country. These 20,000,000 illegals are going to continue to shop for the cheap products because they do not have any pride in America and could care less about our future.

The American way of life can be summed up quite simply: "The bitterness of poor quality is remembered long after the sweetness of low price(s) is forgotten." When we ship our jobs overseas in order to have $300 TV's and $10 shirts we build an inevitable end. How many of you have notices that the "We Support Our Troops" magnetic ribbons you have on the back of your cars are made in China? It is possible to only "buy American" but it takes some work and dedication but it can be done. Put down your Wii's and park you're Toyotas and start working to save our children's way of life.

Thank NAFTA and Bill Clinton, Shame Bill didn't tell everyone when he signed on to this that they would all need new skills, didn't prepare his people for what they were facing. He did not tell us, this means all the big companies will be moving to foreign countries for cheap labor, that our jobs producing products would be gone. That we would be importing most of our products, that we would not be doing much exporting and I don't recall him explaining global economy, Obama is now telling school children that they need to learn new skills for the global economy. Stop buying Imports, Demand that our government only sign Contracts with companies that produce products that are made in the USA. At least if we go under, we'll do it fighting. We far outnumber the super rich.

What I find more disgusting than anything else that is sold in the United States of America are the American Flags that are made in a foreign country. Everyone needs to look at where the next flag you are buying is made and never purchase one that is not "Made in the USA". If you want to purchase an American Flag you can contact your representatives in Congress and they will show you where to purchase the real flag.

All of the buzz and paranoia in the United States about China is a sign of the times. It comes down to a sense of insecurity and of envy. With our own economy in the tanks, and likely to stay there for a while to come, people are fearing that we have seen the end of "American greatness" and the death of the American dream, and all of this while having to look at China's booming economy. Even the state of our mutual military situations is part of it: for the last decade Americans have had to see their military, in which we take so much pride, being handed humiliating defeats by rag tag militias. So to see China's rapidly expanding and strengthening army is a source of envy and insecurity. And I also think, to some extent, there is some nostalgia involved as well. Many Americans yearn for a simpler day when we just knew who "the bad guys" were, and we knew how to handle them. Of all people, John Stewart put it best when he did a joke report last year after a group of Russian spies were apprehended on US soil, saying that the Pentagon reaction was probably "Thank God! Something we understand, no Arabic, no deserts!" and that "Capturing these Russian spies is like recapturing a piece of ourselves!"

What is America going to do? Are we going to remain on this free trade path to destruction, or are we going to demand our politicians do away with all free trade and have fair trade and protect our people, our jobs and our way of life? We only have 2 choices. How did we get in this situation? It is due to corporations being able to buy our politicians with campaign contributions through lobbyists. It's either of and for the people or of and for the corporations.

Things won't change until we make fundamental changes in Congress. We need business leaders in Congress not lawyers who wish to debate something until hell freezes over. You have a front row seat to the death of America as we know it. It's time to protect America and take care of Americans and do what's best for this country and not Mexico or China.

We have a major problem in the election of our representatives to Congress. The businessmen that would have the knowledge and skills to run the government are too busy making billions for their corporations and are not interested in the political garbage that goes on in our government. Unfortunately, that leaves the lawyer vultures scrambling to get into office for a lifetime of entitlements. These lawyers truly believe that it is better than chasing ambulances to

locate someone they can represent to file a lawsuit against someone else.

"Economists foretell of United States decline, China's ascension" Hell, we all knew this back in the early 1990's when Vice President Al Gore used his odd tie breaker and deciding vote to pass NAFTA in a fast-track voting scheme that wouldn't listen to the overwhelming majority of the United States population that opposed NAFTA and GATT. Since then it was a no brainier?

THE CHANGE THAT AMERICA NEEDS

The supporters of the American Citizens Political Action committee are going to present the peoples ideas to the members of the Congress. The people of the United States have made it clear that the 112th Congress had better think about what is happening in our country and take action to return the United States to the people and forget about the foreign countries. Repeal the free trade policies such as NAFTA. Impose tariffs on all imported products that enter the United States. Place an excise tax on all corporations that outsource jobs to a foreign country to make the labor markets competitive. It is perfectly clear. Do what the people want and stop catering to the foreign countries. Bring our jobs home and stop purchasing the junk from China and any other foreign country.

PROGRAM ELEVEN:

THE TREND IN DEMOCRATIC POLITICS

The American Citizens Political Action Committee wants every citizen of the United States to take the time to figure out what is causing some states to succeed and others to fail. Then we need to accept the policies that are successful in the states and apply those policies to the federal government. At the present time the federal government is applying the policies that fail as the policy for the United States. Consider what is happening in Washington and contact your representatives to make sure we start taking back America from the path of destruction that is heading down.

The American Citizens Political Action Committee is including the following article so that the citizens of the United States can see what has happened in Illinois. This is typical Democratic politics and has already spread into the federal government. The tax and spend policies do not work. Illinois is a good example of what many of the other states are experiencing due to their spend, spend and more spending policies of the majority of the states that are controlled by the Democratic Party. America needs to wake up and make changes to the federal governments policies of operating with a deficit every year. Without a balanced budget we are not going to survive.

Illinois faces a 66 percent tax boost amid budget crisis.

By DEANNA BELLANDI, Associated Press Deanna Bellandi, Associated Press

SPRINGFIELD, Ill. – Democratic Illinois lawmakers beat a looming deadline and approved a 66 percent income-tax increase in a desperate bid to end the state's crippling budget crisis.

Legislative leaders rushed early Wednesday to pass the politically risky plan before a new General Assembly was sworn in at noon, taking a slice out of the Democratic majority and removing lame-duck lawmakers willing to support the tax before leaving office.

The increase now goes to Democratic Gov. Pat Quinn, who supports the plan to temporarily raise the personal tax rate to 5 percent, a two-thirds increase from the current 3 percent rate. Corporate taxes also would climb as part of the effort to close a budget hole that could hit $15 billion this year.

"Governor Quinn today thanks the Illinois General Assembly for taking strong action to confront our fiscal crisis and provide the revenue and reforms needed to stabilize the budget, pay our bills and jumpstart Illinois' economy," a statement from his office said.

Quinn's office said the higher taxes will generate about $6.8 billion a year — a major increase by any measure. In percentage terms, 66 percent might be the biggest increase any state has adopted while grappling with recent economic woes.

It will be coupled with strict 2 percent limits on spending growth. If officials spend above those limits, the tax increase will automatically be canceled. The plan's supporters warned that rising pension and health care costs probably will eat up all the spending allowed by the caps, forcing cuts in other areas of government.

Other pieces of the budget plan failed.

Lawmakers rejected a $1-a-pack increase in cigarette taxes, which would have provided money for schools. They also blocked a plan to borrow $8.7 billion to pay off overdue bills, which means long-suffering businesses and social-service agencies won't get their money anytime soon.

House Speaker Michael Madigan, sounding weary, said Republicans should have supported some parts of the plan instead of voting against everything.

"They're on the sidelines. They don't want to get on the field of play," the Chicago Democrat said. "I'm happy that the day has ended."

But Republicans noted they were not included in negotiations. They also fundamentally reject the idea of raising taxes after years of spending growth.

"We're saying to the people of Illinois, `For eight years we've overspent, now we're going to make it your problem,'" said Rep. Roger Eddy. "We're making up for our mistakes on your back."

The increase means an Illinois resident who now owes $1,000 in state income taxes will pay $1,666 at the new rate. After four years, the rate drops to 4 percent and that same taxpayer will then owe $1,333.

Republicans predict the tax eventually will be made permanent.

"It's a cruel hoax to play on citizens to say this is temporary," said House Minority Leader Tom Cross, R-Oswego.

Democrats bristled at being blamed for the state's financial problems, although they've controlled the governor's office and both legislative chambers since 2003.

They said some of the problem began under Republican governors and that Republicans backed some budgets that increased spending. They argued the national recession sent state revenues into a nosedive and that Democrats already have cut spending by billions of dollars.

"This mess is a mess that is the responsibility of all of us as Republicans and Democrats, of several different governors and part of the mess isn't even anybody's fault," said House Majority Leader Barbara Flynn Currie, D-Chicago.

The new tax money will balance the state's annual budget and let officials begin chipping away at the backlog of unpaid bills. Borrowing money, and then repaying it with a portion of the tax increase, would have allowed those bills to be paid immediately, aiding organizations that provide services for the state but go months without being reimbursed.

The delay and the spending limits are "very troubling" to those groups, said Sean Noble, policy director for Voices for Illinois Children, a member of the statewide Responsible Budget Coalition. Still, he called the tax increase "an enormous step" toward putting Illinois on sound financial footing.

The proposal passed the House on Tuesday night 60-57, the bare minimum. No Republicans backed the measure there or in the Senate, where the measure passed 30-29.

The governor has refused to discuss the tax proposal publicly, although his aides say he supports it. During his election campaign, Quinn promised to veto any tax plan higher than his proposal for a 1-point increase.

Republicans accused Democrats of doing irreparable harm to Illinois families and businesses. Business leaders decried the proposal as a job-killer.

"Based on this particular legislation the only businesses that will benefit are the moving companies that will be helping many of my members move out of this particular state," said Gregory Baise, head of the Illinois Manufacturers' Association.

Democrats countered that even with the increase, Illinois' tax rate will be lower than in many neighboring states — Iowa's top rate is 8.98 percent, Wisconsin's is 7.75 percent. They also maintain that without more money, state government may not be able to pay employees by the end of the year. Major government services might have to be halted, they warn, and groups waiting for state payments will go under.

Spending limits were added to the plan to win the support of some suburban Democrats. Republicans said the limits don't do enough to clamp down.

The limits allow next year's spending to increase considerably so the state can make its required contribution to government retirement systems, pay overdue bills and cover other costs that had been shoved aside. After that, however, spending could not grow more than 2 percent annually for the next three years or else the tax increase would be reversed.

"We're really trying to handcuff ourselves and the governor in our spending," said Illinois Senate President John Cullerton, a Chicago Democrat.

The comments that follow are from the citizens of the United States. It is great to know that the average American understands the problems that Illinois is facing but the politicians are not able to understand the problems. Why are they continually elected to keep on making the same mistakes? The state of Illinois has been controlled by the Democrats and their back door policies for many years and this is what happens.

The Democrats in Illinois have robbed and raped that place so much that they have to raise the taxes by 66%, is that a sign of bad management? Then look at how many governors have been put in prison for fraud, or impeached and where did Obama live and who did he appoint to his administration recently? Watch Illinois lose a lot of people who are fed up with the place and move out, what is the reputation of Chicago but a mob agenda?

I am from Iowa and have lived all over the country (military and college). I live in Illinois now. I have never seen stupidity on this level anywhere in my 41 years as I have in Illinois over the last several years. But that's the way it is when these Chicago liberal slobs are in control. I can't leave due to my job. Guess I will be spending less on products and services. That's good for businesses isn't it?

Wow a sanctuary state for illegals going broke, how surprising.

Well there you go the home state of Obama, wanting to raise taxes, got to start somewhere, good luck Illinois.

Check out New Jersey! Under a new Republican Governor who is taking on the unions there they have decreased the unemployment rate, made the projected multi-billion deficit disappear and took care of the snow without a hitch!! Try it. You'll like it.

Lived in Kankakee for 20 years and watched as 1,000's of jobs were lost as the factories closed and moved to states with less oppressive tax structures. This also caused the home values to decline. When I finally saw my chance and bailed out too and the last 20 years I have been right next door in Indiana. Lower State Tax, Real Estate Tax, lower gas prices, lower Sales Tax, etc. Glad to be gone as will several 100 businesses and several 1,000 workers over the next 5 years.

The Slimming Down of Illinois has begun but Illinois will most likely maintain it's reputation as one of the "Most Politically Corrupt States in the Nation!"

Where are all the Illinois people that love and voted for big government. You love it so. Your big government can take your money and spend it for you because they are smarter than you and care more. Your big government can solve all the problems and help anyone who is a victim. Someday you are in for quite a shock when you realize that your big government doesn't create jobs, doesn't grow the economy, doesn't help people, and is inherently broken. Until then, keep up defending your government and big spending lawyer politicians.

I wonder why states with the highest income tax also have the highest rate of debt. Maybe it's just a coincidence?

Maybe all public and government workers should have their benefits and pensions reduced first. Taxpayers should not have to support their early retirements with increasing taxes. And all government should have to work to normal retirement age 65+ like most private workers.

Now that the census is over, we can increase taxes enough to force the massive move out of the state and the resultant loss of revenue, jobs and opportunities that will eventually occur. Why is it that politicians can be so willing to raise taxes before making any attempt to cut spending?

Some of the counties that elected Quinn 60% of the voters can't speak English. Illinois. What a liberal cesspool. The United States needs to look at this type of activity and make the English language a requirement of the United States. That all ballots be printed in English. If the voter can not read, then they should not be voting.

Talk about stupid move after stupid move. You're going to find out just like California will, you make your state to expensive to do business in and the businesses will simply pull out and relocate. Once the manufacturing jobs dry up the real hurt is going to kick in. What do you expect when you vote Democrat?

Here's one instance that Republicans are totally on target about unions. Can you even imagine the debt that has piled up in the Chicago area over the years due to the pensions and perks?

I do think that they should go over all their budgets and programs to trim the fat there...maybe they should look at the incomes they pull in...Do they really need six figures? If they can give themselves raises on a regular basis while the rest of us get put off on raises due to these hard economic times - that the companies we work for say they cannot give us - that would set better than squeezing the little people even more so that they don't have to feel that pinch.

This is the perfect example why Americans are so upset with the way things are in this country. You have governments spending, spending, and more spending, and when the well starts to dry, well, lets take some more. It is sickening to see this. Government's idea to balance budgets that are ridiculously high as it is is to suck all the blood out of turnip it can. Government is asking for big time trouble.

Tax and spend tax and spend tax and spend.......Illinois has been dominated by tax and spend Democrats for eons and yet they continue to get elected. Same is true for California and Massachusetts which are all places I will not live. I have no idea what it takes for you folks to wake up, maybe you are all just comatose and it is too late.

States all talk about budget deficits but never publish the states detailed fiscal budget numbers. In the corporate world every dollar

that is spent is accounted for. The states and federal government have made budgeting this so arbitrary they just throw numbers out there with annual increases based on previous years. There is no oversight on trillions of dollars in spending for military programs, intelligence services, and other secret government programs. Not to mention the payoffs to foreign countries (100's of billions every year!) The concept of fiscal responsibility is a complete canard.

Here comes the Obama led Democratic predictable tax tsunami. First California, now Illinois and there are several other states ready to pull the tax trigger. When will people ever learn? Democrats raising taxes is their modus operandi to pay for all the dysfunctional "we are the world we are the children" policies and programs. They always portray themselves like Robin Hood but are always the worst Sheriff the town ever had. Just despicable!

Has anyone figured out that every state that is going belly up is Democratic? Guess where our president comes from and what a disaster he and his commie buddies left behind. More importantly what kind of a disaster is Obama going to create in Washington?

When are the bonehead Democratic voters going to realize that the big Democratic states are bankrupt and the Republican states are doing well? How hard is this to see?

Isn't it interesting that United States citizens must decrease spending when we have a budget shortfall? Yet the government simply demands more dollars from its subjects. I don't think they have gotten the message they should have received from the last election.

The American people have no more to give. We employ you politicians to look after our welfare and you only look after your own. We are struggling to pay our bills while you greedy pigs are living high on the hog. We are dying from lack of healthcare while you receive full healthcare for life. A 5.25% state income tax may not seem like a lot, but when you add it to the other local taxes and fees, the other state taxes and fees, and the other federal taxes and fees, We the People have nothing left. You all are living better than every one of your employers! You are public servants! Do any of you nitwits truly understand what that means? Let's see how many of you would really be interested in serving the public when you are required to work at normal wages? You vipers are insatiable. Start by cutting the cost of government first. There is so much that we the people don't need or want but you legislate any way. You have bureaucracies so entrenched that you have us thinking that they are vital to our welfare, but they are only vital to your maintaining power. You are supposed to be working for the people, but more and more, we are working for you. We have nothing more to give. We have nothing more to give. We the American people, have nothing, absolutely nothing, else to give!

Is anyone else noticing that the states with "progressive" governments are all broke, raising taxes, and trying to cut benefits?

Will anyone make the logical connection to federal spending before it's too late? Will anyone recognize that the only ones guaranteed to benefit from government programs are politicians and government employees?

My in laws live in Illinois and want me to move there. Ha! Fat chance I would ever leave Texas where we have no state income tax. Oh, we have Republicans in charge here and have had for a long time. Has anyone figured out that every state that is going belly up is Democrat?

"The trouble with socialism is that eventually you run out of other people's money." Margaret Thatcher

The democrats are making themselves irrelevant for at least the next decade. In 2012, the only political support that party will have will be the illegals and non working welfare recipients. 66% tax increase! How about reducing the amount of welfare recipients in the state by 66% instead?

The new governor of Wisconsin is going to cut spending and at the very the worse freeze taxes. Illinois is raising taxes by 75% and if history is a guide this will be permanent and raising corporate taxes. Again history screams out that Wisconsin will see revenues increase while Illinois will remain massively in debt. How many times must it be pointed out to reactionary Democrats that tax increases do not increase revenues?

Meanwhile, next door in Indiana, the Republican Governor who

refused bail-out money from Obama is projecting a budget surplus. Yep, it must be all those selfish, greedy, evil, barbaric rich people who are responsible for all our countries woes.

Why stop at a 5.75% tax? Illinois should increase the tax rate to 30%. The people of Illinois won'[t mind. They love giving their tax money to corrupt politicians. In Chicago, for example, they wouldn't have it any other way. And these days, times are tough! The economy is so bad in Chicago that the Mafia had to lay off two federal judges, one circuit court judge, and three municipal judges. Somebody has to pay for the growth of crime, corruption, waste, fraud, and mismanagement, and the taxpayers of Illinois have been selected! They should pay their taxes proudly, even if it destroys them.

Jumpstart the economy! That's a good one. I'm glad Quinn is able to find humor in the Illinois government's deplorable condition. Stealing an additional 2% of every individual's income is certainly a great way to "jumpstart the economy." It will keep people from doing foolish things like saving for the future or purchasing necessities.

Well if they are going to raise taxes from 3% to 5.25% on people who go out everyday and earn a living then they need to cut the welfare payments by the same amount to those who do not work at all. That way everybody helps fix the problem.

It's hilarious how politicians applaud each other for raising taxes. They really seem to think it is work they are doing. I'm sure they will enjoy finding new and creative ways to spend the new revenue they have just decreed.

Poor dumb Illinois citizens. You get what you deserve for continually voting corrupt imbeciles into office for years on end and sucking up to the corrupt union bosses. No sympathy from this Texan who pays 0% state tax, 6.25% sales tax in a state with unemployment at 6% and running a budget surplus.

Is it a coincidence that the states of New York, California, Michigan and Illinois are among both the most liberal and the most financially strained? A pox on every sheep that voted for Obama! His "liberal

paradise" model has gone nationwide. Expect worse schools, higher taxes, stricter gun laws (except for criminals) and a host of other problems.

This is the same political crap that Obama and the Chicago crew are trying to bring to Washington. Vote them all out if their election committee will allow them to.

Attention Liberals, Obama Socialist and progressives. Illinois is calling you. Break out your bank books and move there immediately. Go support the people who don't want to work. In fact why don't you take California and New York along with Illinois and separate yourselves from the rest of the country. Form your own tax me to death country and leave the rest of the hard working peoples pay checks alone. Tax and spend then tax and spend some more is all you idiots know. How about work, cut expenses from government, start with Obama and his cronies and work your way down. By the way while you're at it cut the middle class people's taxes by 25% so they can live without supporting you bums.

Here's an idea, cut the pensions of state workers. Let them live like the rest of us without the parachute when they retire. Your pension fund is ruining your state...idiots!

Anybody out there who still doesn't understand why there's a Tea Party movement in this country? Except the politicians of course!

You people would not listen to what the conservatives have been warning you what was coming. All you did is call us bad names and tell lies about us. This is your reward for your brilliance of choice in a liar blowing smoke up your rear end, well never mind. It happened because you are stupid. Thank you for infecting the rest of the nation with Chicago politics.

First Illinois is a crooked corrupt state... Chicago is the worst... It supports thousands of worthless welfare chiselers, mostly blacks who all vote for Obama.... It is mismanaged and full of bribes, kickbacks etc...Now the liberals are about to find out the true color of Obama. And the democratic party.... black with a white stripe...So, let's hear your big mouths now...... loyal liberals that you are...Wait. I know...

blame Palin or Bush or the Republicans for your stupidity...Just remember.... you voted the crooks into office and don't have the guts to throw them out....Illinois taxes are among the highest in the nation and now you will pay 66% more.

The Texas Constitution requires the Legislature to balance its budget every year without borrowing against future receipts. That bars the government from deficit spending and forces lawmakers, who meet for 20 weeks every two years, too constantly balance demands for programs and services against voters' desire to limit taxes, fees and other costs of government. So say what you want about the Texas budget for 2011 having a deficit, Texas lawmakers will cut spending to balance the budget.

I live in Illinois and they have no business whatever increasing the taxes at this point; they have done nothing about the pensions, cutting personnel or programs (in fact Quinn gave his employees raises), overhauling welfare, or any of the other cost cutting measures that have been recommended to them by a number of organizations and the citizenry. Chicago (Cook County) was the only area that elected Quinn, everyone else voted for Brady, but no one in Chicago wants the free ride cut off and Democrats need the votes, so they will take this tax increase and run with it and spend it in whatever way pleases their base. Unions were exempt from any cuts until mid-2012 by Quinn, so they're home free. However, it's time for the politicians and legislators to fish or cut bait; they and their employees need also to be squeezed like the rest of us. I'm fortunate to still have my job, but we employees haven't had a raise in 5 years, have received no company match to 401K, my property taxes have almost doubled, gas, groceries, and everything else have gone sky high and all they can think of is how to tax more, never think that it is they and their uncontrolled spending that are the problem.

Maybe if they didn't have such generous benefits they'd have a little more skin in the game, it's easy to spend someone else's money, but they've reached the point of no return. Businesses and people will leave in droves, and who will be left to tax?

If nothing else, the Democrats are consistent...they operate the same at the federal level and state level. Take from those that produce and spend on those that don't.

It is unfortunate as I live in Illinois. But Illinois citizens with their genetic predisposition to vote Democratic deserve this medicine. The life will teach lessons, eventually. And yes, the neighboring states welcome Illinois businesses, especially, Indiana.

Is everyone starting to notice a pattern from Democrats to blaming everyone but themselves, this should be a warning for the Obama's administration? Unfortunately, the Obama administration does not listen to anything that the citizens of the United States are telling him.

So Illinois is about $7 billion in debt with a few more in unpaid bills. The Democrats solution is to tax you 5% of your income. Then another 10% for local sales tax, property tax......so they are into these people just in the state for lets say 17% of all your income. Don't blink now because Uncle Sam wants his 33%. Then we need to include all the utility taxes they pay, phone, internet, Gas, oil...you name it. I say you're being soaked about 45 % of your income. Now you have to pay the mortgage and rent. That is no solution to anything, stop spending & start firing city workers, stop all pensions and feed into a 401K. Maybe even a 15% across the board pay cut for all state employees. You have to do something other than raise taxes.

The state income tax rate will revert back to 3% just as soon as the toll ways are converted to freeways and pigs figure out how to fly. They can't afford to run the state now on a 3% tax, so how are they going to do it later on unless they find ways to reduce expenses, not just keep them from increasing more than 2% per year? This type of program only makes sense to the Democrats.

In my Crystal Ball I see Businesses and Citizens fleeing Illinois and going to low tax states. The Democrat Politicians have only one way of thinking, Tax and Spend. This leads to taxpayers and businesses leaving and going to lower tax states. If they were serious they would cut expenses and graft but they would rather water at the public trough. Pretty soon there will only be politicians and welfare people left in Illinois and no tax base.

I hope this is the final straw and that people realize what Obama is trying to do to us nationally. Saul Alinsky would be so proud........what a failed regime!

Here's an idea, cut the pensions of state workers. Let them live like the rest of us without the parachute when they retire. Your pension fund is ruining your state...idiots!

OUR REACTION TO THE CITIZENS

Did anyone notice that the Democrats passed this legislation in Illinois at the last minute possible to make sure that the Republicans who were elected to office did not have a chance to stop the bill? This is a typical Democratic move to jam legislation down the throats of the citizens of Illinois. Looks like Obama and the Democrats learned the political system well. That is what the Democrats practice all the time in Washington. I sure hope the new 112th Congress changes that policy.

America needs to wake up and take a look at what is successful and what doesn't work. It is not surprising that the states that follow fiscal responsibility, limit entitlement programs, cut spending and support having a balanced budget are not facing the problems of California, Illinois, New York, Michigan and many of the other states that have been controlled by the Democratic Party for years.

The following is lesson on economics:

The Governor of California is jogging with his dog along a nature trail. A coyote jumps out and attacks the Governor's dog, then bites the Governor.

1. The Governor starts to intervene, but reflects upon the movie "Bambi" and then realizes he should stop because the coyote is only doing what is natural.

2. He calls animal control. Animal Control captures the coyote and bills the State $200 testing it for diseases and $500 for relocating it.

3. He calls a veterinarian. The vet collects the dead dog and bills the State $200 testing it for diseases.

4. The Governor goes to hospital and spends $3,500 getting checked for diseases from the coyote and on getting his bite wound bandaged.

5. The running trail gets shut down for 6 months while Fish & Game conducts a $100,000 survey to make sure the area is now free of dangerous animals.

6. The Governor spends $50,000 in state funds implementing a "coyote awareness program" for residents of the area.

7. The State Legislature spends $2 million to study how to better treat rabies and how to permanently eradicate the disease throughout the world.

8. The Governor's security agent is fired for not stopping the attack. The State spends $150,000 to hire and train a new agent with additional special training re: the nature of coyotes.

9. PETA protests the coyote's relocation and files a $5 million suit against the State.

How Wyoming solves the same problem.

The Governor of Wyoming is jogging with his dog along a nature trail. A Coyote jumps out and attacks his dog.

1. The Governor shoots the coyote with his State-issued pistol and keeps jogging. The Governor has spent $0.50 on a .45 ACP hollow point cartridge.

2. The Buzzards eat the dead coyote.

And that, my friends, is why California is broke and Wyoming is not.

PROBLEM TWELVE:

THE LABOR UNIONS

The labor unions that are controlling the outrageous salary demands and high cost of government in the United States need to be eliminated. If the United States government is not going to treat their employees properly it is a disgrace to the country. Why do we need unions for government workers? All they do is raise the cost of operating the government. The same employees should be required to perform their duties in a professional manner without a union bargaining for them. What ever happened to doing a good job to earn the salary that you are receiving? The unions are what have caused the salary level of government workers to be approximately 2.5 times higher than what the private sector is paying for the same services.

An example of how President Obama and the unions have ripped off the American citizens. The unions and the constant demand for more wages and benefits are the major part of what caused General Motors to fail.

President Obama probably does think this was a success because it fits his socialist agenda and is working just as he planned. The government screwed the shareholders and bondholders out of their money when General Motors declared bankruptcy and now all my union buddies are rich, boy this is so easy when the sheep bury their heads in the sand.

Sorry no. The rise in General Motors stock does not validate the President despite his claim. Of course if the stock of GM sinks next week, he will then run, hide and then blame Bush and claim he had nothing to do with the bailout.

Obama your insane! You policy helped the unions. This is another Obama scam. Ask a GM bond holder or a retirement plan who had invested heavily how this helped them. Obama please take your lying liberal self and take a long walk on a short pier.

United States taxpayers will get back 25 cents on every dollar we gave General Motors. The UAW Union will get $4 billion dollars without having to invest any money into the company. Who is this a great deal for?

I'm not sure which is greater, President Obama's ignorance or his arrogance.

How is it that union auto workers average $55 per hour including pensions, insurance? No way that in a free market you can get $55 per hour average for what amounts to unskilled labor. If Obama wants to do something for America, abolish the UAW and let the auto manufacturers open up their doors to anyone without a union card willing to learn the trade.

Obama allowed Government Motors to forget about a $65 billion dollar tax obligation. It's so much easier to look like a success when you don't have to show a real accounting for what you have wrought, especially when it's on the taxpayer's dime. You need to wake up America. The President has pulled a bag over your head so you can't see the light.

Let's discuss this in a few months. How did the UAW end up with 4.8 million shares of stock while the American people's value was diluted? What in the hell did they do for this gift; besides getting Obama elected? This stock in General Motors is expected to peak at $38-$40/share, institutions will sell off, individual citizens will get in and get end up holding the bag as usual. Do not buy this stock. If you want to invest in an automotive stock buy Ford. Then go out and buy a Ford Truck. Ford did it the American way; they bailed themselves out the old-fashioned way.

The American Citizens Political Action Committee hopes that

the unions are going to be extinct within a few years. That will be the biggest improvement in our unemployment situation. A good operating company would be able to hire more employees at the same or lower cost and improve the quality of the products. People need to understand that when they have a job it must be done properly and on time or they can be fired. The unions do not operate on the same principle.

State and municipal officials need to take on unions to cut public spending, freeze salaries, cutting pensions and inhibiting collective bargaining to address the budget shortfalls in their government. The large percentage of the state and municipal governments are on the brink of bankruptcy.

The popularity of labor unions takes a hit when the economy is bad and unemployed workers look on with envy at the more generous wages and benefits commanded by unionized workers. Today's resentment toward unions is a new phenomenon that stems from the decades long decline of union membership and the increase in the unemployed.

This is the most disgusting problem that the country is facing. About 92 percent of the union members are working for the government which includes the school systems, local government, state government and the federal government. The government organizations are supposed to be run for the benefit of the taxpaying citizens and not the benefit of the unions.

In government unions and their counterparts in private-sector unions are living in different environments. Private sector union members now frequently pay for their own health care and have defined-contribution pension plans like 401(k)s. The public sector union members are rewarded with contracts whose pension and health care provisions now threaten many municipalities and states with bankruptcy.

Government employees are responding to this crisis by demanding more and higher taxes. This situation will only make more people who have money less inclined to look to those states to make the investments that create jobs for, say, iron workers, electricians and construction workers.

Government employees should accept a wage freeze in return for salary hikes once the economy recovers, request bonuses for better service or greater productivity, agree to contribute more to their health insurance policies, and replace their defined-benefit pensions with Social Security and supplemental defined-contribution plans, as in the private sector.

Crippling the public sector unions would seriously cut into a major funding source for the Democratic Party. Conservatives succeeded spectacularly over the past few decades in destroying private sector unions and in the process did considerable damage to the Democratic Party in the process.

What Will Replace Unions?

Marxian rhetoric in general, about class or rent extraction or the balance of power between capital and labor, is treated with great suspicion by the broad mass of the population.

Meanwhile the people who control capital are willing and even eager to take money they would otherwise use employing middle class Americans, and spend it on cheaper and equally productive workers abroad.

If the era of the union is over, as it seems to be, what other countervailing force will work to preserve the value of labor?

It's not clear what type of institution can work at an international level to restore the bargaining power workers have lost with the decline in unions, but it is clear that something like this is needed.

PROGRAM THIRTEEN:

DEFENSE SPENDING

F-35 looking more like white elephant

by Mathieu Rabechault t – Thursday January 13, 2011

WASHINGTON (AFP) – The F-35 fighter jet, set to replace a large part of the US warplane fleet, has become the most expensive weapons program ever, drawing increased scrutiny at a time of tight public finances.

Following a series of cost overruns and delays, the program is now expected to cost a whopping 382 billion dollars, for 2,443 aircraft.

The so-called 5th generation fighter was built with features designed to help avoid enemy radar and ensure American supremacy in the skies for decades.

But there is now the potential for competition from China, which this week unveiled its first radar-evading combat aircraft and fueled a sense of a military rivalry between the two powers.

At home, the Lockheed Martin F-35 is getting increased criticism even from some at the Pentagon.

Defense officials say the original cost estimates have now doubled to make each plane's price tag reach some 92 million dollars.

At the same time, the contract awarded in 2001 had been planned to last 10 years, but has been extended to 2016 because of testing and design issues.

Lockheed Martin, which is working with Northrop Grumman and BAE Systems, is developing three versions of the aircraft, which are being designed for ground attack as well as reconnaissance missions.

The F-35A is designed to replace the F-16 and A-10 of the US Air Force, while the F-35C is designed for deployment on aircraft carriers to supplant to F-18, and the F-35B would have a vertical takeoff capacity and replace Harrier aircraft.

US Defense Secretary Robert Gates has warned the cost overruns cannot continue and expressed particular concern over the short take-off and vertical landing variant.

"The culture of endless money that has taken hold must be replaced by a culture of restraint," he said recently.

For the short-takeoff version, Gates has ordered "the equivalent of a two-year probation," adding that "if we cannot fix this variant during this time frame and get it back on track in terms of performance, cost and schedule, then I believe it should be canceled."

As part of a cost-saving drive, the Pentagon chief has decided to delay the purchase of 124 of the 449 units of this version until 2016.

Another bone of contention is a second engine being developed for the fighter by General Electric and Rolls Royce in case the Pratt & Whitney engine is not up to par. Gates contends this second engine is "unneeded."

Private analysts say the whole F-35 program is becoming a money pit.

"The incredibly unfortunate phrase 'too big to fail' applies to this aircraft more than any other defense program," said Richard Aboulafia, an aerospace industry analyst with the Teal Group.

"It's difficult to think of a civil or military program in the past decade that hasn't experienced similar delays and cost overruns."

Still, it may be hard to make many changes to the F-35 program because Britain and seven other countries have been closely involved in its development.

The United States is covering 90 percent of the cost of the development but has participation from Britain, Italy, Turkey, the Netherlands, Canada, Denmark, Norway and Australia. Other nations, including Israel and Singapore, have signed contracts to buy the plane.

"The US wants a globalized JSF program for a combination of strategic and economic reasons," said Aboulafia.

The American Citizens Political Action Committee is in favor of developing the weapons and systems that are vital to the future protection of the United States. The costs are astronomical but a necessity. We believe that cost over runs should be limited and a complete accounting of what the funding was spent for should be provided before any additional funds are allocated. The comments of the citizens are as follows.

The United States is covering 90 percent of the cost of the development but has participation from Britain, Italy, Turkey, the Netherlands, Canada, Denmark, Norway and Australia? This is exactly what's wrong with are economy we give it away to everybody else. 8 countries want it made and we pay 90% of the cost to have it made. We spend billions of dollars to protect 95% of the world from the other 5%, and then we're to politically correct to use any of them to solve the problems. And let's not forget more importantly that we also send 90% of the troops and suffer 90% of the casualties. Let the rest of the world take care of their own boarders and we'll take care of ours.

It takes the Marines 4 hours to swap out a F18 engine. It takes a private civilian UNION Contractor 4 weeks to do the same job and 3

times the help. I consistently see these union workers sitting on their butt's playing cards and counting all the overtime they are putting in. Why do you think these new aircraft cost so much? Obama's union thugs. Our military needs top notch equipment. I work on a military base and see the crap the military has to keep running. They need new gear so give it to them. One of these days we will wish we did.

For one this should be built as a fighter and recon only. To think that this would make a good ground support replacement for the A-10 is ridiculous. There are many reasons why the A-10 is such a superb ground support platform. Chief amongst these is its durability. A-10's can withstand tremendous damage and still keep the pilot safe and make it back home (in some cases even continue the mission). The A-10 follows in the foot steps of another plane built by the same company that was called the P-47 Thunderbolt, or as many called it 'The Juggernaut' with it's ability to be almost impossible to shoot down. Also close-ground support planes that have high stall speeds (such as Mach capable fighter jets) will be less effective in the role of ground support, they simply fly too fast to be able to make target determination and as a result will either not spot targets or they will be the cause of friendly fire incidents. The A-10's engines are spaced far apart for a reason, so that one engine is a still able to function in the event of a hit to the other engine (it's called redundancy folks). The design of this plane does not allow for this very important feature. The Raptor is already a platform that will guarantee air superiority, yet it's cost would prohibit mass production, this is the role that the F-35 was to fill, as it was intended to be a lower cost fighter that could be produced en-masse and would also allow the US to share (ie; sell) it with our allies while keeping the Raptor to ourselves. So let's build it as it was intended and stop trying make it in to something it should not be.

President Eisenhower warned us of "the military industrial complex" long ago. We've seen with our own eyes Big Business, especially Big Finance (Insurance is included here) runs America. President Franklin Roosevelt made a most striking statement on that topic long before Eisenhower in a letter dated Nov. 21, 1933 to Edward Mandell House (Google him and read up on him. You learn interesting stuff). "The real truth of the matter is, as you and I know that a financial element in the larger centers has owned the government ever since the days of Andrew Jackson."

House did indeed know; he was one of the "financial element" and key proponent of the Federal Reserve Act, especially as Pres. Woodrow Wilson's right hand man and top adviser. Wilson, as you might know, signed the Federal Reserve Act into law. Of this, Congressman Charles A. Lindbergh Sr. said, "When the President signs this Act, the invisible government of the monetary power will be legalized...the worst legislative crime of the ages is perpetrated by this bill."

That's why it doesn't matter which Party is in office. They are OWNED. The ONLY reason they are getting concerned about the "endless money" is that the source of the endless money is getting wise to scam and very pissed off.

$382 BILLION for fighter planes? Every nation needs a defense system. However, why does the U.S continue to believe that they are fighting the Cold War, and the threat to the U.S will come in the form of a tank and or an invading army? The greatest threat to the U.S and its future is, you're $14 trillion in debt. Your educational system is falling apart. The U.S is falling way behind other industrialized nations when it comes to science and mathematics, which is crucial to any nation that wishes to lead the technological world. Your cities and infrastructure is eroding. Your total reliance on foreign oil and imports has turned you into a "dependent nation". Your corporate America has sold you out. Their outsourcing all your best jobs and have turned your manufacturing industry over to China and India. As of right now, your country is in deep trouble. You may be able to prevent an invading army on your soil, put you can't stop the loss of your country if you continue down the path you're on.

There is nothing wrong with the jets out now. Upgrade the radars, power plants, and avionics and you have a brand new plane with a 10th the cost. Or make 2011 versions of the aircrafts. There is no reason for 2000 of anything new all at once. One squadron will suffice to work out all the kinks and gradually build the squadrons up. Besides, the government is allowing these companies to rape their wallets. Set a peak limit to manufacturing cost and profit and call it a day.

Maybe ... and this is just a suggestion, the US government should include in the contract clause when they order these planes that if the companies building the planes have cost overruns, the companies should eat some of their profit.

The advanced avionics in the planes is what makes these projects so expensive. The ability to detect aircraft and other targets at a greater distance and have targeting solutions long before the enemy detects these planes. They can fire their ordinance and get out of dodge before anyone knows whets coming. The technology to save pilot's lives is in this plane and it does cost allot of money. People want a military to protect them but are willing to sacrifice more pilots to save a buck? The government is charged with protecting the country first and foremost, not making sure Johnny has a laptop or to protect a teachers salary. Everyone thinks the military is a waste...until something happens. Everyone has short memories. Cut and paste articles like these really make me angry. Every tank we have ever developed had cost overruns.

The Left says this about every weapons system ever developed. We were told the Apache helicopter was so trouble plagued, that if it was deployed it would be useless as it would spend all its time getting maintenance. We were told the M-1 Abrams tank could not function in a dusty environment, that it was such a fuel hog it couldn't be deployed, that it had such a large IR signature it would be an easy target for heat seeking weapons. Instead what we saw was their complete dominance of the battlefield.

What is the alternative for the F-35? The F-16, F-18 and F-22 productions lines are being shut down. The F-15 production line has been shut down for almost a decade. The F-117 production was stopped decades ago. The B-2 bomber was stopped at 18 aircraft. There are only about 60 available B-1 bombers and the B-52 fleet is down to about 50 aircraft. The A-10 production was stopped in the late 70's.

Simple, the contractors are just bleeding the taxpayer's money, senators and congressman's that benefits from it are channeling the money to their district. The contractors should shoulder the expenses for any modification. These contractors should be held responsible for delaying tactics. It's just like those auto mechanics at the dealer charging you when they cannot diagnose the problem right away and make mistakes. Plain and simple RIPOFF.

The F-35 has no 30mm Vulcan, can't carry many of the munitions an A-10 can, and nothing can take more damage than an A-10 and make it home. It can't be replaced.

The F-22 can carry the same bomb load of an F-35 and conduct strike missions, but the F-35 can't match the F-22 in the air superiority role. Naturally we cut the operational F-22 for the F-35 in the bush. They'll probably do like they did with the B-1 and B-2, pay for the whole run, only take delivery of a small fraction, and then pretend to be shocked by the unit price.

Don't our political leaders realize that we are supporting the military growth of these nations with the help of American corporations building their economies and not the good old U.S.A. Slam the door on imports or at least make it an equal trade agreement. The United States needs to have $1 billion in imports from foreign countries for $1 billion in exports from America. We didn't have this prolonged problem when local state and the federal government were required to purchase made in the U.S.A. Wake up its getting late!

PROGRAM FOURTEEN:

THE NEXT RECESSION?

The economists are predicting the next recession will be caused by the continued number of foreclosures in the housing market, the federal deficit, spending out of control, oil prices reaching levels above $132.00 per barrel and the unemployment situation which is predicted to hover around the 10% level for the next few years. They fail to mention the drain on the resources of the United States that is caused by the 20,000,000 illegals that are in the Country.

The American Citizens Political Action Committee has been supporting policies that will address the same issues that the economists are concerned will cause the next recession. Where do these economists come from thinking that the country is actually out of the last recession?

When the oil prices reach $132.00 per barrel the citizens of the United States are going to see the price of regular gas reach an average of $4.50 to $5.00 per gallon at the local pump. That is going to place an enormous strain on the buying power of the average American. It will mean that the prices of food and all other staples are going to increase in relation to the price of oil.

WHAT ARE THE SOLUTIONS?

The solutions are what we have been trying to get the members of the 112th Congress to pass legislation for the programs that will start to resolve these situations. The American people seem to have a much better grasp of the problems that we are having then the politicians that we have elected to represent us. That is where the real problems are and we are not getting any action to solve them.

The solutions are not going to be easy because the problems have been ignored for so many years. The American people are very strong and they will adapt to the changes required to save our great country just like we have for the last 200 years.

We have to make sure that the politicians that are representing us are going to make the decisions that are not politically correct and legislate for all the citizens of the United States. By the way, illegals are not citizens of the United States and there is no such thing as a Mexican-American.

Taking back America has to be every citizen's top priority.

OUR NATURAL RESOURCES

When we produce the oil and natural gas from the resources of the United States we will provide for the countries vast consumption but we will decrease our national deficit each year. How simple can it be? We need people with common sense in Washington and not people with Doctors Degrees. History has shown that some of the most highly educated individuals do not have one iota of common sense and are not able to listen to what the American public wants. The truth about producing our natural resources is following.

Not everyone is against the production of our natural resources. Some are just clinging to the past. Oil has been produced for about 80 years. Other sources of energy are in fact expensive when you compare it to oil. And that's why no one really wants to do it right now. But eventually we will have to do it because we will run out of oil. I honestly think solar is the way to go. However, it's a very limited resource. It's only good for a few things whereas oil can be used for over 6000 different products throughout the world.

Oil is the energy source in our lifetime. Stop and think about that for a moment. It is the source of energy in our lifetime. We need oil, we must have it. It is the source of so many products. Did you know plastic requires oil? Oil is here to stay. At least in our lifetime it is. I understand that in the future other energy sources will take over but for now oil is king.

The Gulf oil spill is a good example of the misinformed leading the misinformed. I hope everyone who thinks this way can afford to pay $10.00 per gallon for gas. You have been lied to by the militant environmentalist movement. The spill, while regrettable, certainly could have been minimized if our leaders would have taken the proper steps to solve the situation early. The truth is they wanted it to be this bad so that they could further their agenda to bring America to its knees through the green movement. The Obama administration gave British Petroleum 274 passes on failed safety inspections in the last year alone. So who is really at fault? You won't hear about these facts being reported by the main stream media. The main stream media is blinding you and they haven't had to work very hard to accomplish the fact. They lie straight to your face yet you are too lazy to go get the facts yourself.

Information gathered from the biological, seismic and geological studies was used to complete a Legislative Environmental Impact Statement (LEIS) that described the potential impacts of oil and gas development. This LEIS study included the Secretary's final report and recommendation, and was submitted to Congress in 1987. The report concluded that oil development and production in the 1002 Area would have major effects on the Porcupine Caribou herd and muskoxen. Major effects were defined as "widespread, long-term change in habitat availability or quality which would likely modify natural abundance or distribution of species." Moderate effects were expected for wolves, wolverine, polar bears, snow geese, seabirds and shorebirds, arctic grayling and coastal fish. Major restrictions on subsistence activities by Kaktovik residents would also be expected. In the report, the Secretary of Interior recommended that Congress authorize an oil and gas leasing program that would avoid unnecessary adverse effects on the environment.

Congress failed to act on the recommendation, first in 1989 following the Exxon Valdez oil spill, and again in 1991 when a provision to open the Arctic Refuge to development was dropped from the National Energy Policy Act. In 1995, Congress passed budget legislation that included a provision to allow drilling in the Refuge. Citing a desire to protect biological and wilderness values, President Clinton vetoed the bill.

The estimated oil reserves in the Artic Refuge's 1002 Area are in excess of 30 billion barrels that could be recoverable. With oil prices over $80.00 per barrel and going higher it would be in the best interest of the United States to commence drilling in this area. These reserves would reduce the national debt and provide the United States with independence from foreign oil producers. Every barrel of oil that the United States can produce eliminates one that has to be imported.

Newer technologies that are applied today in Alaska's expanding North Slope oil fields include directional drilling that allows for multiple well heads on smaller drill pads; the re-injection of drilling wastes into the ground, which replaces surface reserve pits; better delineation of oil reserves using 3-dimensional seismic surveys, which has reduced the number of dry holes; and use of temporary ice pads and ice roads for conducting exploratory drilling and construction in the winter. As the oil fields expand east and west, additional oil reserves are consequently being tapped from smaller satellite fields that rely on the existing infrastructure at Prudhoe Bay and Kuparuk.

FORECLOSURE PROBLEMS

The foreclosure crisis is not going to help any of the homeowners that are facing foreclosure get refinancing so that they can remain in their homes. The issue is about the creditability of the lending institutes in their processing of the loan documents. The whole mess was caused by realtors, appraisers, mortgage companies and the governments mandate that every American should own a home. This was first implemented by the Carter administration and then given steroids by the Clinton administration.

The idea that every American should own a home is ludicrous. When someone wants to own a home they need to know how they are going to pay for the home. What ever happened to the requirement of a reasonable down payment? How about proof of income so that the lending institute will know that you have the means to make the payments? What about back up funds in case of emergency or termination from employment? These questions were not being asked because no one cared. Then the loan documents were transferred to another lender and the paperwork did not always follow. The lenders became lax and didn't read the majority of the documents to see if they were in order and rubber stamped their approval.

The lending institutes really were after making the profits from the initial filing fees and could have cared less about whether the loan would be repaid. They knew that they were going to sell the loan to another mortgage company and then the next mortgage company would package the loan with others and sell them to Fannie Mae or Freddie Mac. They were under the impression that they were off the hook for the mortgage.

If the homeowner had done what the mortgage and banking industry has done they would be accused of fraud and embezzlement and prosecuted to the fullest extent of the law. Why can the mortgage and banking institutes practice these fraudulent procedures they get a free ride and are not prosecuted? What happened to everyone being equal before the law? The abuse of the law by politically powerful banks undermines one of the key tenets of the American way.

Deutsche Bank National Trust filed to foreclose on a homeowner even though it had sold the mortgage to Goldman Sachs. This would mean that it did not have any legal right to foreclose. One judge found that about half of the motions filed in his court were so full of errors that he refused to approve them.

The documents that are filed in court are the foundation of our legal system. A signed affidavit is legally equivalent to providing live testimony in court. If an affidavit is untrue, that's the same as lying in court, which is a crime called perjury.

Yet the current system is filled with thousands of cases where the banking industry used documents that were fraudulently submitted to the court that were certified as accurate when they were in fact not. Attorneys are prohibited from making a material misrepresentation to the court, it's clear that such misrepresentations of fact are widespread in foreclosure proceedings.

In the good old days, when a bank issued a mortgage they would hold the loan as an asset and collect the interest and principal payments from the homeowner. But Wall Street banks divided the payments that go toward interest and loan principal into slices, which were assembled by risk and rate of return into pools of mortgages that were then sold as a single security. With the mortgages divided into pieces that were then bundled into securities that were bought and sold numerous times, the ownership of the underlying mortgage and home often became muddled. This is how two different companies can end up filing foreclosure documents on the same house.

Every time this type of securities changed hands, the various claims on the underlying house should have been transferred as well. In many cases, they weren't. In some cases, foreclosures have been allowed even when the original mortgage has been lost. If you don't need the original document to take someone's home, then exactly what rule of law is at work in America?

The flawed foreclosure documents are going to drag out the housing slump for several years. The uncertainty of not knowing how many foreclosed homes are going to be on the market is going to continue to drag the home prices even lower. The sale of foreclosed homes is going to be severely damaged due to the integrity of the documents. Why would anyone want to buy a home not knowing whether the legal documents could be adequate to provide title insurance?

With millions of foreclosed homes on the market that cannot be sold with clear titles, then that will effectively freeze a significant portion of the American real estate market. After all, about a third of all home sales involve residences in default or foreclosure.

Fannie Mae and Freddie Mac have been pulling foreclosed homes off the market, canceling signed deals and removing properties from inventory of unsold homes. Homeowners already in the foreclosure process are now wondering whether the impending foreclosure situation will delay or even cancel their impending eviction notices.

Most Americans have not trusted the lending institutes for many years with regard to their fairness and maneuvering of the legal system for their benefit. The points system and closing costs created huge profits for the lenders. All were demanded up front to provide the banks with substantial profits.

The foreclosure problems are going to last for several years and the economy is going to be held back from a quick and sustained recovery. The housing market and jobs are the key factors that are going to keep our economy improving at a snails pace.

COST OF ILLEGALS

The government needs to hire enough employees to enforce the laws and not allow any more illegals into the United States. We have the resources to locate and deport all of the illegals. We find it amazing that during the mad cow epidemic our government could track a single cow, born in Canada, almost three years ago, right to the stall where she slept in the State of Washington and they tracked her calves to their stalls? But they are unable to locate 20 million illegals when they wander around our country. Maybe we should give each of them a cow so that we can locate them?

When the illegals are deported from the United States make sure that they are finger printed at the border. Prepare a data base regarding all the deported illegals. The data base could include a picture and a DNA sample. Anytime one of the illegals returns and is caught they will go directly to jail for five (5) years.

The government should announce that they will be employing a policy to give the illegals a thirty (30) day window to voluntarily leave the United States or face deportation. Anyone that voluntarily leaves will be allowed to return legally with the proper documentation.

The United States needs to pass legislation that will eliminate all the wasted money printing documents in Spanish. English is the language of the United States. If people can not read the material printed in English, then they must learn English. You do not go to any foreign country and expect their government documents to be in English. It is absurd that our voting ballets are printed in two languages. We must eliminate the idiotic policy of having to press 1 for English and 2 for Spanish.

The United States must send the millions of illegals back to the country that they came from. President Eisenhower was the last president to deport somewhere around 12,000,000 illegals and he was one of the most respected presidents in history. Our current administration needs to read the constitution and understand that America is the home of the free and the brave for those that choose to come here legally. Nowhere does it indicate that you can come here illegally. All the illegals need to be deported and take their anchor babies with them.

We need to stop worrying about the rights of these illegals. By entering the Unites States without the proper legal documents they immediately become felons. They are felons and should be treated as such.

The Homeland Security Department that is headed by Janet Napolitano has an internal memo that is designed to give amnesty to the majority of the illegals in the United States. The memo reportedly will allow this measure to bypass Congressional approval. We can not let this type of policy be enforced in the United States. The majority of the people do not want amnesty of any kind. Why don't the Democrats listen to what the people want?

When will the American people start to look at some of the facts concerning the invasion by 20,000,000 illegals that are destroying the true American way of life? We are going to present some information about what is happening in the United States right now.

How can any branch of the United States government even think about giving this type of person amnesty to become an American citizen? That is absurd.

ABOLISHING THE UNIONS

We will be stirring up a hornets nest with this one. All the unions should be abolished. They are ruining the United States of America.

We received a message from one of the supporters who is 86 years old. He has been a union member all his working life and believes that the unions have out lived their usefulness. A few days ago, the media reported that the Unions were going to donate $50 million to support the Democrat candidates during the mid-term elections on November 2, 2010. This is nothing but a payback for all the money that was given to bail out General Motors, Chrysler and the many other companies that are dominated by union workers.

One example of the extreme favoritism provided to the union is General Motors. The unions received 17.5% of the new GM after their bankruptcy filing and the United States government received 62%. Had General Motors abolished the unions many years ago they would not have had the problem and requirement of the government to bail them out. The union wages and benefits are atrocious. GM could have hired 2 or 3 workers that wanted a good job for every union worker at a much lower cost. That $50 to $60 per hour plus benefits is one of the major reasons that General Motors failed.

Everybody knew it was ridiculous and unsustainable to pay workers indefinitely not to work (in the United Auto Workers union's Jobs Bank), and to pay gold-plated pension and health-care benefits to employees. But all of these practices, paid for by mounting debt obligations, continued for decades in GM's 30-year, slow-motion crash. It is incredible that General Motors still use union workers instead of hiring people that want to work and produce better products for less money. No wonder they needed to be bailed out by the government to the tune of about $65 billion of taxpayer money.

The businesses that hire union workers should fail. They are putting up with the unions and when an employee does not do the work they are protected by the unions. It is time that employers look at what is produced by each individual and base their pay their productivity. If they do not produce what is expected, then they should be fired.

The unions were needed when they were first organized. Unfortunately, they have abused the system and should be abolished.

Not to mention the latest $30 billion bail out that was primarily for the benefit of union organizations. Why do the teachers need a union? They should be in the teaching profession to educate our young people. If they are having problems with providing the proper education they should not be protected from losing their jobs because they are union members. Currently, teachers are making more than millions of other working Americans.

The relevant question looking forward is whether the unthinkable—going broke—also could happen to America.

PUTTING AMERICA TO WORK:

We do not believe that the real unemployment rate is 9.8%. How is it possible that the government reports the unemployment rate at these levels?

The unemployment rate that the government has been reporting does not take into consideration the facts that unemployment has ran out for several hundred thousand workers with thousands more running out each week. These people have been dropped from the statistics and are no longer counted in the unemployment rate. They simply do not exist anymore to the United States government's thinking. How convenient it is to make the statistics look much better than they really are. Not to mention that they factored in the hiring of over 400,000 part time census workers to make the picture look brighter.

When you consider all the people that have had their unemployment benefits expire, add the people that have taken a crappy part time job which takes them off of the unemployment rolls and just the millions of workers that have just given up because there are not enough new jobs created the unemployment rate in reality is more like 20% of the working people of America. There are 6 unemployed workers for every 1 job posting. The unemployment picture was not improving so the

government gave the unemployed an additional 99 weeks of benefits at the expense of the tax paying citizens.

The United States needs to create about 400,000 new jobs each month to keep up with the expanding population. We are going in the wrong direction. Business leaders will not hire new employees until the economy shows major signs of improvement and the uncertainty of the healthcare costs and the Bush tax cuts are extended. The present administration can not get the Bush tax cuts extended until he gets off his stupid position of not extending the cuts to people who earn over $250,000. These are the people that will be creating most of the new jobs that the country desperately needs. It is unfortunate that our leader is not able to understand economics 101.

There are about 16,000,000 plus illegal Mexican's working for peanuts and not paying taxes in the United States. Remove these back to there home country and ours will have many more jobs. Repealing NAFTA would also be a great start to creating jobs in America.

We feel that God should be part of everyone's lives and that any American can prey anytime that they desire. There should not be any separation of God from the United States. All of our money makes this statement. Look at every dollar bill. It will contain "In God We Trust". Why are so many people against prayers in our school system? This just does not make any sense.

TRADE DEFICIT

The United States needs to reduce the amount of products imported from countries that are taking advantage of minimum wages and destroying the buy "Made in the USA". One way to make the prices of our products comparable with the imported would be to implement a surtax of 40% on all foreign products that retailers are selling in the United States. This tax could be calculated on their purchase invoices from the foreign country and would be easy to compute.

The critics will scream that it will raise prices. Yes, it probably will. Wouldn't it be better to pay a little more and get a product that is "Made in the

USA" and improve this countries ability to manufacture more goods? By bringing the manufacturing jobs back to the United States it will create more employment for the American citizens.

Everybody knows that we're running unsustainable federal deficits. That Fannie Mae and Freddie Mac created financial sinkholes by helping lenders make mortgages to people who couldn't afford them. That many states' public-employee pension funds are hopelessly under funded for the level of benefits they provide. That shoveling more money into the public schools without insisting on structural reforms and accountability hasn't produced results and won't do so in the future.

Addressing these issues inevitably means enforcing spending discipline and standing up to public-employee unions in a way that GM failed to do with the UAW. Continued denial and delay will prove ruinous. To put it another way: America bailed out General Motors, but who will bail out America?

The IWW organization has spoken out against NAFTA against labor abuses. They are already complaining that the wages are too low. Representatives of the IWW used a PowerPoint presentation in West Philly, Pennsylvania to illustrate their testimony, they spoke for two hours about the poverty, repression, and environmental health disasters that NAFTA is causing in Mexico's industrial belt. Photos of poverty-stricken slums, polluted waterways, deformed animals and dangerous factory conditions demonstrated the dire situation that Mexican workers and their families face on a daily basis.

Meanwhile workers paid poverty wages that require a factory worker to spend three hours to earn what an undocumented immigrant worker in Los Angeles makes in twelve minutes. These conditions make massive immigration across the border to the United States inevitable.

Is there any wonder why we predict the quality will go down and that more illegals will be trying to get into the United States of America? It needs to stop now.

SPENDING OUT OF CONTROL:

An Entourage that is Unbelievable:

You may have already read about this in your local newspapers. Oh no, you didn't? OK then, you saw in on CNN or the main stream media. No? I didn't think so. Those outlets are too lame to publish or broadcast real stories about their fair haired leader Obama. You and I may never see health care again the way it used to be, but "Emperor Obama" took six (6) doctors with him on a three (3) day visit to London. Not to mention the other 494 member essential staff.

You have to love this spread the wealth vote for change operation. This is while he says he is going to freeze government employee's salaries for two years. The money Obama wasted on this trip could have paid the majority of these salaries for about a year. Obama just keeps on wasting the taxpayers money like it is his personal bank with no limits on the spending he does for personal reasons.

President Barack Obama proposed a two-year freeze of the salaries of some 2 million federal workers, trying to seize the deficit-cutting initiative from Republicans with a sudden, dramatic stroke. Though signaling White House concern over record deficits, the freeze would make only a tiny dent in annual deficits or the nation's $14 trillion debt.

Would you like to see what "Big Government" implies? Take a look at the following information that was published by Dale McFeatters, a writer for Scripps Howard News Service concerning Obama's trip to the G-20 summit in London, England.

President Obama arrived at the G-20 summit in London with everything but the kitchen sink. He did however bring the White House chef and the entire kitchen staff.

The heads of government are in London to discuss serious and weighty issues. The news is not focused upon the Obama entourage that landed in London for the summit.

Obama arrived with a staff of 500 including 200 secret service agents and a staff of 6 doctors. Obama had to bring his own water and food. No wonder the rest of the heads of government were laughing. Obama also shipped 35 vehicles to London and brought along a staff of 4 Speech writers and 12 Teleprompters. It appears that Obama is going to have plenty to say at the summit. To bad it will not be what he really believes but what his lackey speech writers prepare.

Then since Obama could not use his Beast, which is Obama's eight ton armored car that just returned from Asia, to get from the Stansted Airport to Central London the government had to ship his private helicopter the Marine One and a fleet of duplicate decoy helicopters to take him from the airport to downtown. You talk about gall. Obama and his ego are the biggest laughing stock of the entire world.

THE TRUTH ABOUT OBAMA'S FREEZING PAY ON GOVERNMENT EMPLOYEES:

President Obama's proposal of a pay freeze for federal employees is a small step towards curbing government spending. However, a closer look shows there is less to it than meets the eye. In fact, many federal employees will still see their salaries increased.

While Obama's plan would stop the annual across-the-board cost of living adjustment for all federal workers, it will not stop government workers from getting raises altogether. The freeze will not affect pay raises for job classification upgrades. Employees will still be eligible for step increases. Step promotions also known as within grade increases are mandated by statute. They are nearly automatic as long as an employee performs his job adequately. Within grade increases shall be effective on the first day of the first pay period following completion of the required waiting period and in compliance with the conditions of eligibility.

Here's how the system works. Over 70 percent of the federal workforce (except for the military and postal workers) is paid according to the General Schedule or GS pay scale. The GS pay scale includes 15 wage grades that reflect the category and skill necessary to perform a job, with 10 steps within each grade.

New employees can expect to receive a step increase every year, mid-level employees every two years, and senior employees every three years. Step increases can range from $728.00 for a GS 3 to $3,321.00 for a GS 15. Grade increases can range from $2,214.00 for a GS 1 to GS 2 to $14,931.00 for a GS 14 to GS 15. These numbers represent the 'base' amount for federal pay. The government gives a percentage increase for different areas of the country to reflect local variations in cost of living.

For example, despite the pay freeze, a government employee living in Washington, D.C., who is classified as a GS14 Step 1 and is upgraded to a GS 15 Step 2, will receive a raise of about $22,500 per year. The next year that same federal employee without a promotion or grade increase can see their pay go up by $4,126 through a step increase.

Even more importantly, the freeze would probably have happened anyway. Increases in federal pay and government assistance are calculated based on rising prices and higher costs. In October, the Social Security Administration reported that there would be no automatic COLA increase for the 58 million Americans receiving Social Security benefits.

The cost of living increase would not affect any of the grade or step increases of the federal employees. Now that these programs are really cutting into the government reducing costs and size. Is it any wonder that once a government employee they want to remain one for life? Legislation needs to be acted upon to curb these abuses of the federal government. It goes back to the good old boys protecting the government employees and screwing the 58 million senior citizens that are receiving Social Security.

President Obama claimed that the freeze would save $2 billion over the rest of this fiscal year and $28 billion in cumulative savings over the next five years. The freeze barely scratches the surface of the real savings that could be achieved if federal employees pay were brought into line with private sector wages.

Federal salaries have ballooned over the last few years and are far greater than salaries in the private sector. USA Today reports that the number of federal workers earning $150,000 or more a year has soared tenfold in the past five years and doubled since President Obama took office

Most of the federal compensation is not a contractual obligation and Congress can reduce it in those positions which are overcompensated. If Congress reduced this federal pay to market rates this would save taxpayers about $47 billion a year.

Union officials have strongly criticized the freeze. The President of the American Federation of Government Employees replied to the freeze as using the federal employees as a scapegoat and a superficial panicked reaction to the deficit commissions report. This one is really good. The AFL-CIO called the freeze bad for the middle class, bad for the economy and bad for business.

How can it be bad for business when the only people that are affected are the government employees? The unions need to understand that the government employees are a burden on the taxpayers and the businesses that hire the private sector. Government employees are paid from the taxpayers.

REAL FACTS ABOUT UNEMPLOYMENT:

There will be no increase in employment until a real fair trade agreement is reached in this country.

As it stands, any manufacturing of durable goods such as appliances, are making a mass exodus from our country to Mexico before the Obama health plan takes affect so they can avoid the onslaught of increased taxation.

Go look at your local Home Depot, Lowe's, Best Buy, Chevy, Ford dealer, etc. and look at where these products are being produced.

Without a strong manufacturing base here in the United States, there is no revenue to sustain our schools, police and fire, roads, or any other tax based programs.

NAFTA was a sham that fitted perfectly into big business interests so what little manufacturing was left here could affordably move out of this country and into countries with little or no tax liabilities, and cheap labor.

It was a very short-sighted attempt at increasing the bottom line for major corporations with no regard for future revenue from the American labor force.

Try imposing taxation on a bottle of shampoo imported from China (look at the label), and see what the Chinese do to counteract this. They will simply fire all the workers currently making $1.25 an hour and replace them with those who will work for $0.75 an hour.

Until we make it profitable for a company to produce a product here instead of outsourcing it to a different country, our entire economy is sunk.

The college educated idiots seem to forget that when they were growing up, there were a tremendous amount of classmates throughout high school that had a difficult time keeping up academically with them, and those are the people that need these manufacturing jobs to sustain their own lifestyles.

Obama and his brethren in Congress (whether that be the Democrats or Republicans) cannot grasp this concept. His answer instead of cutting back and staying within a budget, is to keep piling on more debt, tax all the people more and keep forcing our companies to move to out of country manufacturing facilities.

In order to circumvent paying for the health care legislation, more and more companies are going to be forced to quit hiring full time employees and pay them as private contractors who will be responsible for their own health care, retirement, and other benefits they were accustomed to.

I can't wait to see how many IRS agents have to be hired to extract taxes from all these private contractors to pay the bills that Washington has placed upon our heads. The government is dreaming. These private contractors will then be entitled to all the business deductions that were not available to them as employees of a company. Therefore, they will show less profit and less taxable income due to the business deductions. The government is going to lose more revenue than they can possibly gain.

The November 2010 unemployment rate that was reported by the government was steady at 9.8% with no real signs of any improvement in the near future. Where all of those jobs that were promised by President Obama from his $800 billion stimulus program? They must be miracle jobs that nobody can see or earn wages from.

PROGRAM FIFTEEN:

RESPECT FOR AMERICA:

We will try to address some of our concerns about the direction the United States has gone with regard to the playing of the National Anthem, saying the Pledge of Allegiance to the Flag, the use of the English language and the printing of government forms in Spanish. These areas are problems that are having a major effect on the direction that the United States of America has taken.

We are sure that this will anger all the non-English-speaking people that are living in the United States of America. The human rights groups will be saying we are not American. Good, then maybe we can get some action to correct these problems.

We find it disgraceful that we have to press 1 to talk to some businesses and/or the local, state and federal governments. Eliminate that press 2 for Spanish. If the American citizens want to do business in the United States then they should learn the English language. Is that really to much to ask? Anyone that thinks we are being unfair should try going to some other country and see if they will speak a special language for them. It will not happen.

The American Flag should be flown at every event that the public attends. Then the National Anthem should be played prior to the start of the event. All the people in attendance should be standing facing the Flag with their right hand over their heart and singing along. The National Anthem should be played at every assembly of every school in America and all the children should learn the words. It is a shame that the majority of Americans do not know the words. Everyday, the schools should say the Pledge of Allegiance to the Flag. Again, this will teach all the children the words. It also will instill the beliefs that our Country and Flag are worth protecting and understanding.

Printing our ballots to vote and the government forms in the United States in Spanish is an absolute disgrace and should be abolished. We find it disgusting that we need to pamper people that can not read English. If they can not read, how are they going to understand what they are voting for? It leads to votes that could have been swayed by organizations like ACORN.

These are things that most of the citizens were raised to believe in. It has just been the past several years that we have given up our principles. It is past time that we reinstate these policies.

It is very irritating that the President of the United States has abolished the National Prayer Day and then celebrates the Muslim Holy days. This is a major embarrassment and insult to the vast majority of the citizens. We need to reestablish our rights.

We feel that God should be part of everyone's lives and that any American can prey anytime that they desire. There should not be any separation of God from the United States. All of our money makes this statement. Look at every dollar bill. It will contain "In God We Trust". Why are so many people against prayers in our school system? This just does not make any sense.

THE PRESIDENTS PROTECT THE CHANGE:

President Obama is now creating a new rallying call. "Protect the Change"

Why would anyone in their right mind want to protect the change that

has happened in the last two years? It was really annoying to us that the president made the rallying call to the "Black Caucus in Congress" what a racist remark. Why didn't Obama give a rallying call to all the Democrats instead of catering to the Black and Hispanic voters? There is nothing more disgusting than Obama trying to create division the voters of the United States and doing everything that he can to create a class structure in the United States.

We never thought we would be able to experience what the ordinary, moral German felt in the mid-1930s. In those times, the messiah was a former smooth-talking rabble-rouser from the streets, about whom the average German knew next to nothing. What they did know was that he was associated with groups that shouted, shoved, and pushed around people with whom they disagreed; he edged his way onto the political stage through great oratory and promises. Economic times were tough, people were losing jobs, and he was a great speaker. And he smiled and waved a lot. And people, even newspapers, were afraid to speak out for fear that his "brown shirts" would bully them into submission. And then, he was duly elected to office, a full-throttled economic crisis at hand [the Great Depression].

Slowly but surely he seized the controls of government power, department-by-department, person-by-person,

bureaucracy-by-bureaucracy. The kids joined a Youth Movement in his name, where they were taught what to think. How did he get the people on his side? He did it promising jobs to the jobless, money to the indigent, and goodies for the military-industrial complex. He did it by indoctrinating the children, advocating gun control, health care for all, better wages, better jobs, and promising to re-instill pride once again in the country, across Europe, and across the world.

He did it with a compliant media; did you know that? And he did this all in the name of justice and 'CHANGE'. And the people surely got what they voted for. Read your history books. Many people objected in 1933 and were shouted down, called names, laughed at, and made fun of. When Winston Churchill pointed out the obvious in the late 1930s while seated in the House of Lords in England, he was booed into his seat and called a crazy troublemaker. He was right, though.

Don't forget that Germany was the most educated, cultured country in Europe. It was full of music, art, museums, hospitals, laboratories, and universities. In less than six years, a shorter time span than just two terms of a United States presidency, it was rounding up its own citizens, killing others, abrogating its laws, turning children against parents, and neighbors against neighbors, all with the best of intentions of course. The road to Hell is always paved with them.

As practical thinkers, that are not overly prone to emotional decisions, we have a choice: we can either believe what the objective pieces of evidence tell us (even if they make us cringe with disgust); we can believe what history is shouting to us from across the chasm of seven decades; or we can hope we are wrong by closing our eyes, having another drink, and ignoring what is transpiring around the American citizens.

We certainly do not hope that the change that Obama was referring to is comparable to the above. Although just about everything he advocates indicates he is promoting a class structure in the United States. The American people need to wake up and smell what is going on. As we have read and listened to the rhetoric that Obama has spewed across the nation we need to stop the change and not protect the changes as Obama is asking.

The majority of the Democrats that are running for office all know how to use are the smear campaigns against the Republican foes. That is apparently because they do not have any proposed legislation that will be for the benefit of all Americans. The healthcare program and the stimulus are two examples of passing legislation that the majority of the citizens did not want. We do not need more of the Obama policy of change. It will increase the deficit to incredibly high numbers and Obama has already increased the deficit in 25 months by a larger amount than any other president in their entire terms.

PROGRAM SIXTEEN:

ADDED FOOD FOR THOUGHT:

Professor Joseph Olson of Hamline University School of Law in St. Paul, Minnesota, points out some interesting facts concerning the November 2008 Presidential election:

Number of States won by: Obama: 19 McCain: 29

Square miles of land won by: Obama: 580,000 McCain: 2,427,000

Population of counties won by: Obama: 127 million McCain: 143 million

Murder rate per 100,000 residents in counties won by: Obama: 13.2 McCain: 2.1

Professor Olson adds: "In aggregate, the map of the territory McCain won was mostly the land owned by the taxpaying citizens of the country.

Obama territory mostly encompassed those citizens living in low income tenements and living off various forms of government welfare."

Olson believes the United States is now somewhere between the "complacency and apathy" phase of Professor Tyler's definition of democracy, with some forty percent of the nation's population already having reached the "governmental dependency" phase.

If the government grants amnesty and citizenship to twenty million criminal invaders called illegal - and they vote - then we can say goodbye to the United States of America in fewer than five years.

There was an article about some cities and states that are on the verge of going bankrupt on 2011. When you look at these states you will notice a direct connection to the voting patterns of the Democratic Party. The ignorant are electing a large number of our representatives in Washington. It is past time to stop this.

A recent article about major cities possibly going bankrupt:

This will reinforce the policy of American Citizens PAC that we need to band together and create a policy that will correct these problems within our great country. The Article is as follows:

16 U.S. Cities That Could Face Bankruptcy in 2011

Information provided by the Business Insider, December 21, 2010:

2011 will be the year of the municipal default. At least that's what analysts like Meredith Whitney predict, as do bond investors that have been fleeing the municipal bond market.

There are many reasons to be worried. First, the expiration of Build America Bonds will make it harder for cities to raise funds.

Second, city revenues are crashing and keep getting worse. Property taxes haven't reflected the total damage from the housing crash. High joblessness is cutting into city revenues, while increasing costs for services.

The next default could be a major city like Detroit, or it could be one of hundreds of small cities that are on the brink. Did we leave off your ailing city? Let us know in the comments.

San Diego, Ca.

Projected Deficit through June 2012: $73 million

Budget in Fiscal Year 2011: $2.85 billion

Annualized gap: 1.7%

The city officials have tried curbing the deficit by increasing sales taxes, but residents of the city strongly oppose this and have voted it down.

San Diego already cut over $200 million over the past two years, so these cuts won't come easy.

New York, NY

Projected Deficit through June 2012: $2 billion

Budget in Fiscal Year 2010: $63.1 billion

Annualized gap: 2.1%

Estimates of the New York City deficit range from $3.6 billion according to Comptroller John Liu to around $2 billion according to the Independent Budget Office. Everyone agrees that the deficit will be worse if New York State cuts aid as part of its own deficit reduction plan.

Mayor Bloomberg has already started to address the FY2012 deficit, calling for layoffs in all city agencies, closing 20 fire departments at night, and reducing services for seniors, libraries and cultural centers.

San Jose, Ca.

Projected Deficit through June 2012: $90 million

Budget in Fiscal Year 2010: $2.7 billion

Annualized gap: 2.2%

After an audit of the San Jose police department, city officials found it to have too many high paid supervisors, costing the city too much money. The answer to this is converting some of those upper ranked officers to patrol positions. This could reduce the city's debt by $33 million.

Last year's deficit was $116 million, leading to brutal cuts including nearly 900 layoffs.

Cincinnati, Oh.

Projected Deficit through December 2012: $60 million

Biennial budget Fiscal Year 2009/2010: $2.5 billion

Annualized gap: 2.4%

Helping the budget in Cincinnati depends largely on changes in the police and fire departments. The city can get $20 million in concessions from the two unions, lay off 216 firefighters, or outsource the police force to neighboring city, Hamilton.

Honolulu, Hiawii.

Projected Deficit through June 2012: $100 million

Budget in Fiscal Year 2011: $1.8 billion

Annualized gap: 3.7%

Mayor Peter Carlisle said police officers and fire fighters will be asked to make concessions in the upcoming budget and he will also end furloughs of two days per month for public workers. This will require the 2,900 officers to give back their 6% pay raises they have received in each of the past four years.

Last year Honolulu raised some property taxes to fill a huge $140 million deficit.

San Francisco, Ca.

Projected Deficit through June 2012: $380 million

Budget in Fiscal Year 2011: $6.55 billion

Annualized gap: 3.9%

Mayor Gavin Newsom says this year's deficit is completely manageable. Last year's deficit approached $500 million and the city did not need to lay off any police or firemen. While Newsom's term is coming to an end, he says he and his colleagues will leave detailed options for the incoming mayor.

Last year's cuts were even larger, eliminating a $438 million deficit. The city is down to the bone.

Los Angeles, Ca.

Projected Deficit through June 2012: $438 million

Budget in Fiscal Year 2011: $6.7 billion

Annualized gap: 4.4%

The Los Angeles City Administration Office plans to cut 225 civilian positions in the LAPD, reduce firefighting staffing, and eliminate a dozen positions in the City Attorney's Office and General Service Department. The deficit will only get worse unless an effort to privatize parking garages is approved. If not, the city will require more layoffs, furloughs, and curtailed hiring.

Last year's deficit was even larger, totaling nearly $700,000.

Washington, D.C.

Projected Deficit through September 2012: $688 million

Budget in Fiscal Year 2011: $8.89 billion

Annualized gap: 4.4%

Council member Tommy Wells proposed tax rate increases which were voted down, but Wells says he will continue to push his proposal. Wells' proposal seems reasonable as residents making $100,000 a year would only pay $63 more in taxes per year. This is a small price to pay that would benefit the city immensely.

Newark, NJ

Projected Deficit through December 2011: $30.5 million

Budget in Fiscal Year 2010: $677 million

Annualized gap: 4.5%

Newark's deficit was $83 million before Mayor Cory Booker initiated a plan to sell city-owned buildings, raise property taxes to 16 percent and decimate the police force. Nonetheless, Moody's cut Newark's rating to A3 citing its $30.5 million remaining deficit.

Detroit, Mi

Projected Deficit through June 2011: $85 million

Budget in Fiscal Year 2011: $3.1 billion

Annualized gap: 5.5%

Detroit's city government has cut costs with layoffs and by leaving currently vacant positions open. Mayor Bing's emergency fiscal plan includes demolishing houses and cutting police and trash services to 20% of the city.

Last year the city council pushed through severe cuts to fill an over $700 million deficit.

Reading, Pa

Projected Deficit through December 2011: $7.5 million

Budget in Fiscal Year 2010: $120 million

Annualized gap: 6.3%

One of Pennsylvania's several distressed municipalities, which receive state aid, Reading has been running an operating deficit for years. In September the city council said their deficit was bigger than expected, soaring to $7.5 million for the current year, which means they will have to borrow around $17 million from the state to pay off total debts.

Joliet, IL

Projected Deficit through December 2011: $21 million

Budget in Fiscal Year 2010: $274 million

Annualized gap: 7.7%

Last year, the city increased property tax by over 12 percent and hiked water and sewer rates by 45 percent over three years to help with the deficit. The city council also cut police and public sector jobs.

Camden, NJ

Projected Deficit through December 2011: $26.5 million

Budget in Fiscal Year 2010: $178 million

Annualized gap: 15%

Despite holding title of second most dangerous city in America, Camden recently received approval to lay off half of its police force.

Hamtramck, Mi

Projected Deficit through June 2012: $4.7 million

Budget in Fiscal Year 2011: $18 million

Annualized gap: 17%

City manager Bill Cooper was denied permission to declare bankruptcy. He says the city is owed millions of dollars in tax dollars from Detroit from a shared facility. The state offered the city a loan to stave off bankruptcy.

Cooper says he has already cut almost everything possible, going so far as to lay off the city's five crossing guards.

Hamtramck might avoid bankruptcy, but also-broke Michigan can't afford many of these deals. That's why Gov. Rick Snyder predicts "hundreds of jurisdictions" going bankrupt in the next four years.

Central Falls, RI

Projected Deficit through June 2012: $7 million

Budget in Fiscal Year 2011: $21 million

Annualized gap: 22%

Central Falls has been put in state receivership due to critical budget problems. State-appointed receiver Mark Pfeiffer thinks the best solution is for Central Falls to be annexed by its neighboring city, Pawtucket.

Paterson, N.J.

Projected Deficit through December 2011: $54 million

Budget for Fiscal Year 2010: $225 million

Annualized gap: 24%

As a "last resort," Paterson is considering laying off 30 percent of its police force, said councilman Steve Olimpio. This will put 150 police officers out of work.

BONUS: Chicago, Il

Projected Deficit through December 2011: $654 million Closed

Budget in Fiscal Year 2010: $6.8 billion

Annualized gap: 9.6%

Mayor Richard Daley has balanced the budget, but absolutely ruined Chicago finances from here on.

His FY2011 plan uses up nearly the entire revenue from a long-term lease of the local parking system and airport, which he passed in 2008. The multi-billion lease deal was supposed to last for decades, but it only lasted two years. The best hope for the future is building a city-owned casino

That explains some of the problems that these cities are facing. Now let's address some of the comments regarding these problems. After we review the comments we will consolidate and format a plan on how to solve the systems.

Anyone notice that all the cities listed are Democrat strongholds? Many of these cities have not elected Republicans in 20+ years. The socialist experiment fails again

The writing is on the wall. Look at these cities, mostly large African

American populations with failing school systems, many fatherless children from dysfunctional homes taking their angry, dysfunctional attitudes with them if they even go to school. We as a nation rank near the bottom compared to other industrialized nations in math, science, and languages. These dying cities are just a window into what waits America's future.

But we're America? Nothing bad could ever happen here. The rules of gravity applies anywhere in the world. So do the rules of over-spending. Either you have to cut programs dramatically causing social unrest in many highly populated areas, or we keep printing money and see how long this scheme of "musical chairs" can last. Inflation of 10-20% a year is very probable once the market realizes we are in a much worse position than Europe.

Every city on the list has a large number of welfare programs with lots of illegals and a high percentage of government workers. No wonder they are going broke. When are the American people going to learn?

I find it interesting that 11 of the 16 cities listed in the article are sanctuary cities. Isn't it amazing how much change the illegals bring into the economy?

There is a correlation that all of these cities have and that is they are all liberal and controlled by Democrats. What a surprise? I guess that tax and spend programs are not working so well. Most of the cities on the list also have a high illegal population taking resources that cost the cities money. Deport the illegals and balance you budget.

We live in Port Huron which is just north of Detroit. Port Huron has now become a welfare city. This is because Detroit woman are moving here and having kid after kid and we are giving them free housing, clothing, food, medical, schooling, gifts. All they have to do is parade around there trophy babies and ask for a handout. We will be the next city of the list. Michigan is considered a welfare state, we no longer kid ourselves. 75% moved here from Detroit, Flint and Pontiac and they know a "sucker city" when they see one! We must stop this giving money for more kids. What are we all nuts? Let them once and for all go to work! In the papers today they say the individuals who want to join the services can not because they can't pass the test that is at the 6th grade level. No wonder the country is broke! They learn the easy way, get a young girl pregnant, don't marry and have a dozen kids and their on easy street. That is where the majority of our taxes are going. To entitlements and we're all falling for it. Not me, I have money, I will help an individual who is trying their best to get back on their feet. The others can just forget about any more entitlements.

Three things are common with all these cities. First, they are all run by liberal democrats who have taxed business out of their area. Two, they are all union run cities which has helped run business out of their area. Three, they are all havens for bloodsucking illegal aliens.

There will be no federal bailouts we made sure of that by putting our guys in charge of the house last November. These cities made their bed, now they can lie in it. Fix your problems or starve. The cities are all heavily Democrat, all heavily union and are all pushing hard for socialism. But I just can't put my finger on why they are all going bankrupt.

There are too many giveaway programs. There is too much reckless spending of money that may not be there in the future. There are too many elected officials who want to put their name on a project at the taxpayer's expense. We could not run our households this way. WAKE UP AMERICA

We extended unemployment to stop the American outrage of illegals working and Americans unemployed. We need to stop the Section 8 housing, free medical, food stamps, etc. paid from American taxes to support illegals. Eisenhower, Hoover and Truman deported illegals years ago. We need to follow the examples of these past presidents and we can do it today.

And even worse than that, there are plain old ordinary folks who can tell them how to correct their train wreck, but no one is going to listen. The American dream is dying because of all the giveaways, and they start in the highest income brackets and go all the way to the newest person to come here illegally. I know, there are people who need help, I get that, really I do. But I had to learn a long time ago, you can't fix it for everybody, you have to pick one or two charities and let someone else take up some slack. One example is Medicaid and Medicare. It

should be for SENIORS ONLY; these tired old veterans of life who have paid their dues, paid their taxes, and took this country to its greatest glory with their blood sweat and tears. Now, when they are coming to a point in their lives when they need an arm to lean on they find out that they have been and are being ripped off by the people who have benefited from all their labor. If you know someone who is at retirement age, don't see them as a burden, thank God for them and what they have made possible for you. Even the people who have come to this country illegally owe them a debt of gratitude, because they are the reason there was ever an "American dream" in the first place. I'm not a senior citizen yet, but seeing how they are treated now, I dread the day I become one.

Stop all your free programs to the illegals in this country. Close the borders you idiots. You are allowing the scum of the earth to walk freely into our country and suck it dry. Start there and work your way up from there. Pack all those illegals up and send them back where they belong. Start trying to make this country great again and you might be surprised how many of us Americans come to your aid.

The US Post Office CEO made $857,000 last year for a bankrupt company. Try that for government cost savings. That is only 10.7% of the $8 billion that the United States Postal Service lost during the last year. Not bad if you are that CEO. If any privately run business operated on that same principal the CEO would be fired immediately. Only in the government can things like this happen. I wonder what his retirement funds are going to equal?

Being a Democrat or Republican politician does not matter. Agreeing with the following list of ten axioms by William J. H. Boetcker should be the litmus test.

1. You cannot bring about prosperity by discouraging thrift.

2. You cannot strengthen the weak by weakening the strong.

3. You cannot help the poor man by destroying the rich.

4. You cannot further the brotherhood of man by inciting class hatred.

5. You cannot build character and courage by taking away man's initiative and independence.

6. You cannot help small men by tearing down big men.

7. You cannot lift the wage earner by pulling down the wage payer.

8. You cannot keep out of trouble by spending more than your income.

9. You cannot establish security on borrowed money.

10. You cannot help men permanently by doing for them what they will not do for themselves.

I could not agree more with all the people here who stated that the cities are those run by liberals. Liberals hate what America has stood for. America is the land of the free and the home of the brave. America is a country that picks itself up by the boot straps when it is down and gets the job done. That is what we did when this great country was formed and again in the depression years and again when we were attacked on Pearl Harbor on December 7, 1941. When the world is in trouble who do they call for help? It is always the United States of America. When the world needs food, money, who do they call? It is always the United States of America. It is high time that the United States of America starts to take care of itself. It starts with going back to the roots that made this country great. A true belief in God, the reason this country was founded and put our trust in Him. When this country remembers from whom all blessing flow, it will again be great.

The best thing these cities could do would be to enter into bankruptcy. Public sector unions have bribed and bought politicians in order to get wages and benefits unheard of in the private sector. These cities could void these contracts and negotiate agreements which would be more in line with private company compensation or better yet, abolish their union work force and turn various services over to private, outside firms. Leaders would do this in a heartbeat. Politicians will never do it in a million years. Leaders want what is best for their citizens. Politicians want power.

It is amazing how IGNORANT governments can be. If I were mayor of any of these cities I would simply say, you will budget 10% less next year than you had this year. Look at the deficits? It would make almost 100% of these cities solvent. I have done it in my home, why can't they? A simple process, go back four years and eliminate any program created since then. It would solve every one of these. I AM SICK OF TAXES GOING UP, STOP SPENDING. In the case of California simply enforce the immigration laws and you won't need to steal money from US Citizens to pay for the schooling, healthcare, housing, food and other services you are providing people that BROKE THE LAW AND CAME HERE ILLEGALLY. Citizen's of this country need to stand up and be counted. Notice how every one of these states have Democrats running the show.

Public employee unions = long term financial ruin. Spending persistently beyond your means = long term financial ruin. Fix those two things = long term financial stability. Only vote for candidates who will fix those two things.

These listed cities and their states have large numbers of welfare people, illegals using services without paying, etc. Deport the illegals. Make those on welfare do something for their money. They can pick up trash along the highway or do janitorial work at the local court house, school, etc for a few hours a week. This would help cut expenses.

This is not surprising because the cities with large populations of poor, large groups of recent immigrants, large welfare costs, large social service costs, large unions running the show, large amounts of fraud and abuse. America as a country and these American cities are finally seeing what decades of deficit spending, giving away too much to too many, and basic mismanagement of budgets can do. Now everyone can suffer because the middle class tax payers finally got sick of footing the bill. With so many losing their jobs we can no longer float the liberal spending spree. It's time to rein in the spending and pay attention to getting everyone back to work. It will take a long time to fix this but hopefully we will learn something from it. Vote out anyone that can't agree to a balanced budget without more taxes. We have to make tough choices in our family budgets and so should the government at all levels.

America is the home of the hand outs. Gee I am having a baby. Now you owe me money, free food, free place to live, free cash. I love this country where I can sit on my fanny while you normal citizens have to go to work everyday. I get to live here for free. If I need some more cash all I have to do is just pop out another kid and maybe sell a little dope on the side.

Every city on this list is a liberal city. Why isn't that a surprise? How do people not realize that when liberals are in power we go bankrupt? Try and remember your life before 2007 was pretty good right? We had 4% unemployment, jobs for everyone then the media convinced us we had problem and liberals could fix it and in 2007 the liberals took over spending in Congress and just 4 years later this country is falling apart. Out of all of these liberal cities failing only one states governor is doing anything about it. Chris Christie from New Jersey and New Jersey has 3 cities on this list. But instead of praising him for trying to fix these liberal cities the lame stream media is attacking him and the unions are sending him death threats and protesting him everyday. It's almost like the media is an accomplice to the bankrupting of America. God Bless Chris Christie in 2012.

A LESSON FOR ALL AMERICANS:

My great great grandfather watched as his friends died in the Civil War, my brother watched as his friends died in WW II, and I watched as my friends died in Korea and Vietnam.

None of them died for the Mexican Flag.

Everyone died for the United States flag and the principles that it stands for.

In Texas, a student raised a Mexican flag on a school flag pole; another student took it down. Guess who was expelled...the kid who took it down.

Kids in high school in California were sent home this year on Cinco de Mayo because they wore T-shirts with the American flag printed on them. Enough is enough.

This message needs to be viewed by every American; and every American needs to stand up for America.

We've bent over to appease the America-haters long enough.

I'm taking a stand.

I'm standing up because the hundreds of thousands who died fighting in wars for this country, and for the United States flag can't stand up.

And shame on anyone who tries to make this a racist message.

Let me make this perfectly clear!

THIS IS the Citizens of the United States country. God Bless America

And, because I make This statement it does not mean that mean that I'm against immigration.

You are welcome here in our country. Welcome to come through legally:

1. Get a sponsor.

2. Get a place to lay your head.

3. Get a job.

4. Live by our rules.

5. Pay income taxes.

6. Learn the English language like immigrants

have in the past.

7. Please don't demand that we hand over our lifetime savings of <u>Social Security Funds</u> to you.

If you don't want to forward this for fear of offending someone, then YOU'RE PART OF THE PROBLEM.

When will AMERICANS stop giving away THEIR RIGHTS?

We've gone so far the other way and bent over backwards not to offend anyone.

But it seems no one cares about the AMERICAN CITIZEN that's being offended!

WAKE UP AMERICA.

If you agree then make sure you let all of your friends read this.

PROGRAM SEVENTEEN:

WHAT DO THE MEMBERS OF CONGRESS SUPPORT?

The American Citizens Political Action Committee would like to know what the representative's views are on the issues and what they are supporting. In addition, how are they going to implement their policies for the benefit of all the citizens of the United States? We need to contact all of our representatives and make sure that they are going to be supporting our policies. If they refuse to inform the people about their plans then we need to make sure our people do not vote for them.

Every citizen needs to email their representatives and get their position and solutions for the following issues:

1. What is your position on the border fence? How do you plan on executing your plan?

2. What is your position on Amnesty for the illegals? How do you plan to deport the illegals? If your position is for amnesty, you can count on losing all of our votes.

3. What is you position on exploring for oil and gas in our vast natural resources that the United States controls? How are you going to go about supporting legislation to lessen our dependence on foreign oil?

4.   What are your qualifications to hold your office in Congress? Could you pass a qualification test on the Constitution of the United States?

5.   What is your policy on supporting a balanced budget? What steps are you going to support to achieve the goal of a balanced budget?

6.   What is your position on passing legislation on banning earmarks? Will you vote to ban them?

7.   What is your plan to address the unemployment situation in the United States? Are you in favor of work projects to help reduce the unemployment?

8.   When you propose legislation are you able to demonstrate how the legislation will be paid for? We do not want to support any politician that wants to add to the deficit.

9.   Will you operate with total transparency concerning any legislation that you propose? When the majority of the citizens express their desire or disapproval on your proposals will you listen to what they want?

10. What is your opinion of the back door policies that have been practiced for the last few years? Are you going to put a stop to these policies?

11. What are you going to do about the annual budget deficit? Are you going to put a stop to the enormous amount of money that the budget contains that is listed under discretionary? The 2011 budget contained about 33 percent that gave discretion to the individual departments. Just cutting the discretionary spending will reduce the budget deficit by 10 percent.

12. What is your opinion on repealing the NAFTA? How are you going to go about repealing?

13. What is your opinion about reducing our trade deficit by imposing a tariff on imports that exceed the amount of our exports?

14. What is your position on the corporations of the United States outsourcing jobs to foreign countries? Are you willing to fight to stop this practice? Would you be willing to propose legislation that will tax the excess imports?

15. What other programs are you going to support? How are you going to implement those programs?

16. What is your opinion on the English language? What type of legislation are you going to propose to make the English language the law of the land?

17. What are your opinions on abolishing the unions? Are you going to present legislation that will make it mandatory that all government employees are non unionized?

Washington and the Unions.

The National Labor Relations Board on January 16, 2011, threatened to sue Arizona, South Carolina, South Dakota and Utah over constitutional amendments guaranteeing workers the right to a secret ballot in union elections. Why is the government always going to sue the states? It just doesn't make any sense.

"The powers not delegated to the United States by the Constitution, nor prohibited by it to the States, are reserved to the States respectively, or to the people." The Tenth Amendment to the United States Constitution.

"The ultimate authority, wherever the derivative may be found, resides in the people alone and that if the federal government got too powerful and overstepped its authority, then the people would develop plans of resistance and resort to arms." James Madison (Father of the bill of rights, 4th President of the United States)

Department of Homeland Security

The Department of Homeland Security is having credibility problems? Who would ever believe such a thing? This is the department headed by Ms Janet Napolitano. While she was Governor of Arizona, she kept complaining to the Federal Government that too many illegal immigrants were entering the state from Mexico. Now she has become head of Homeland Security and immediately announced that things on the border with Mexico are all better. Are they? Hah! The only change has been Arizona's SB1070 which requires local and State police to verify the immigration status of anybody that has been arrested. There's nothing wrong with asking for proof of personal information, because police need to see some sort of ID if they are arresting somebody. Have a valid Arizona driver's license. OK. Have a Green Card or equivalent? OK. Have a passport? OK. There is nothing wrong with the Arizona law SB-1070. It specifically prohibits "profiling" or arresting people for being "brown". Now Ms Napolitano has cancelled the virtual fence. That shows how much she cares about Arizona, the rule of law, and her oath to uphold the laws of the land, including the Constitution. Homeland Insecurity would be a better term for the agency.

The Department of Homeland Security should be abolished immediately. The Department of Homeland Security appears to be taking on the characteristics of the former Soviet Unions KGB or the former East German's STASI. What is happening at our airports is exactly what was happening in the former Soviet Union. The enemy was their own citizens and were spied upon constantly needing special permission to not only travel abroad but within the Soviet Union. The citizens were searched both coming and going to any destination. Citizens were encouraged to spy upon their neighbors and children were told to report on their parents. Sounds like what is beginning to happen in our country. WE ARE NOT THE ENEMY.

Our Federal Government is so clueless it's amazing. Homeland Security cannot even do the relatively simple job of securing our porous borders. All the American taxpayer hears from our over inflated government is one lame excuse after another. It's just plain sickening.

SURPRISE SURPRISE SURPRISE

Do you really know what is in the Obama healthcare bill? If you are surprised by the following you are not alone. What we would like to know is just how the following is anywhere connected to healthcare? If it has not already been repealed we must make sure that it is. There are over 2700 pages to this bill and no one knows everything that is hidden within the bill. This is just one sample of the back door politics that are practiced by President Obama. We the citizens of the United States need to stop these practices.

OBAMA CARE IS WHAT THE DOCTOR ORDERED, OR IS IT WHAT THE UNDERTAKER ORDERED?

WILL YOU BE SELLING YOUR HOUSE AFTER 12/31/2012?

Did you know that if you sell your house after 2012 you will pay a 3.8% sales tax on it? That's $3,800 on a $100,000 home etc. When did this happen? It's in the health care bill. Just thought you should know. THE SALES TAX HOUSE SALES IS GOING TO GO INTO EFFECT IN 2013 (Part of HC Bill). Why 2013? Could it be to come to light AFTER the 2012 elections? A REAL ESTATE SALES TAX! So, this is "change you can believe in"?

Under the new health care bill - did you know that all real estate transactions will be subject to a 3.8% Sales Tax? The bulk of these new taxes don't kick in until 2013 If you sell your $400,000 home, there will be a $15,200 tax. This bill is set to screw the retiring generation who often downsize their homes. Does this stuff make your November 2012 vote more important? Oh, you weren't aware this was in the Obamacare bill? Guess what, you aren't alone. There are more than a few members of Congress that aren't aware of it either.

http://www.gop.gov/blog/10/04/08/obamacare-flatlines-obamacare-

We are concerned with the direction that the economy, unemployment, spending, immigration and lack of transparency with the current administration. It is time that the voting citizens voice their opinions and vote for representation that will vote for programs that are for "We the People, By the People and For the People".

ABOUT THE AUTHOR

I was born in Grundy Center, Iowa on October 21, 1937 and raised in Cedar Falls, Iowa until I enlisted in the United States Air Force. I have served my country for 8 years, 1 month and 6 days and have two honorable discharges to show for it. I am currently raising my 9 year old son as a single parent and living on social security. I have been in the stock brokerage business for about 20 years and an accountant for about 25 years. During the last 10 years I have attempted to help start-up companies to have a method of raising capital. As with all start-up companies some of them made it and the majority of them did not. That is just the nature of the start-up business. Through it all I have kept my sanity and have not lost my ability to think. I have been blessed with reasonable intelligence and have the ability to use common sense. I have written the following books: "A Beautiful America" "America Can Recover" "Bashing Sarah Palin", Proud To Be American" and "My American Dream". For more information on my views and photos visit my websites:

www.thomasmeinders.com

www.americancitizenspac.com

www.my-american-dream.org